THE ENDURING

COMMUNITY

THE ENDURING COMMUNITY

Embracing the Priority of the Church

WRITTEN BY BRIAN HABIG & LES NEWSOM

REFORMED UNIVERSITY PRESS

THE ENDURING COMMUNITY

Copyright © 2001 by Reformed University Press

Published by Reformed University Press
(A Division of Reformed University Ministries–Mississippi)
618 Briarwood Drive, Suite A
Jackson, Mississippi 39211

Scripture taken from the Holy Bible, New International Version. NIV Copyright 1973, 1978
1984, by International Bible Society. Used by Permission of Zondervan Publishing House.
All rights reserved.

ISBN 0-9711-0040-3

Reformed University Press is a registered trademark of Reformed University Ministries–Mississippi.

Book layout and design by Carl Fox

Library of Congress Control Number 2001117574

Printed in the United States of America

2001–First Edition

10 9 8 7 6 5 4 3 2 1

To our beloved brides,
Dana and Ginger

Contents

Preface

Back in 1972, a group of committed but relatively modest Presbyterian ministers began an attempt to insure that America's college campuses would have a church-based, Reformed witness. Today, this effort has flowered into Reformed University Ministries (RUM), known on local campuses across America as Reformed University Fellowship (RUF).

There are now upwards of seventy RUFs nationwide. God has blessed the effort and vision of pioneer leaders including Mark Lowrey, who founded RUM in the state of Mississippi.

Now, more than a quarter of a century later, a new need has become obvious. The Joint Committee on Campus Work for Mississippi, West Tennessee, and Arkansas, working with the blessing of RUM at-large, has launched Reformed University Press (RUP), which will produce written materials to serve not only our campus ministries' students, but also the growing number of lay people in the PCA and beyond who trace their spiritual roots to their days in an RUF.

This first book, *The Enduring Community*, is no coincidence. On the contrary, we believe it is the culmination of much prayer and faith-based effort and of a sovereign God's blessing.

This book is the first in a series that RUP intends to produce. This first series will tackle what are considered the fundamentals that we in RUM teach our students: The primacy of the Church; of Scripture; and of the doctrines of Justification, Sanctification, and Glorification.

Campus ministers Brian Habig and Les Newsom, themselves standing on the shoulders of two earlier generations of campus ministers, have written this present book to encapsulate what has, for years, been orally communicated to our students and graduates: that God's Church universal and church locally are His ordained instruments for Christians to grow and for God's work in the world to be accomplished.

We commend to you this work. We believe in it not because we believe in ourselves, but because we believe in God, Who has shown Himself faithful to this doctrine of the Church over the years—this "ecclesiology", to use a theological term.

You will notice a few things in this book: First, we always lowercase the word "church" when referring to a local body, and uppercase "Church" when referring to the larger, non-local body. Second, we have not skirted some teachings that will provide fodder for what we hope to be constructive conversation concerning just what roles God ordained for the Church.

Ultimately, we trust and pray that this book, as all future RUP books, will move your heart and mind to praise God our Father, from Whom all blessings flow!

James "Bebo" Elkin
RUP Director of Publications
Jackson, Mississippi

Acknowledgements

Brian Habig would like to thank the Rev. Scot Sherman of Intown Community Church in Atlanta, Georgia, for insightful feedback concerning the submission of the church. Special thanks to Mr. David C. Hastings, Jr. for reading early drafts and providing helpful suggestions. Brian would also like to express appreciation to the Rev. Brad Stewart and the congregation of Grace Presbyterian Church in Starkville, Mississippi, for their role in his family's life. In very real ways, they have modeled the reality of the body of Christ.

Les Newsom would like to thank Philip Levy and Kelly Shannon for helpful editing comments; to Way Rutherford for a listening ear while "hashing it out"; to Dr. Knox Chamblin and Dr. Dan Doriani for helpful clarifying conversations on the nature of Kingdom and Church; to the Rev. Mo Leverett, Director of Desire Street Ministries in New Orleans, Louisiana, for his vision and input regarding the role of the deacon in a church's life; and to the congregation of Christ Presbyterian Church, Oxford, Mississippi for enduring four months of Sunday nights on the doctrine of the Church.

Brian and Les would like to thank James D. "Bebo" Elkin, Area Coordinator for Reformed University Ministries in Mississippi, who, providentially, was the first to introduce us to the priority of the Church; and also (how could we forget?) the entire staff of campus ministers with Reformed University Ministries. You are our dear friends and true brothers in the faith.

1

The Disappointment of the Church

If you do not want to go to church, you may be in good company.

The reasons vary, but the net result is the same—the local church is often not the priority that it used to be. Describing the local church's perceived importance these days as "diminished" is something akin to describing the status of New York City as "inhabited."

The evidence of this perception is all around. One writer states that, toward the close of the twentieth century, churches in North America and Europe were losing approximately 7,600 participants *every week*.[1] To bring it a bit closer to home, a relative recently commented: "We can't build doors big enough to accommodate the people leaving our church right now."

What is striking about all this is that it does not reveal disappointment on the part of those *outside* the Christian community, but rather, of those *within*. Professing Christians are often—at best—confused about what the local church means for their spiritual growth; they are—at worst—altogether frustrated or disillusioned with it, even to the point of abandonment.

As this trend unfolds, two extremes are possible for people still wanting the local church to "count for something" in our day.

Extreme One

The first extreme is (appropriately) to listen to the voices of frustration and to note what the sources of that frustration are, and then (questionably) to tailor a local church scenario that avoids all possible land mines of frustration. The ultimate example of this in our day is the consumer-driven megachurch.

To be a very large church is not necessarily a problem, in and of itself—Charles H. Spurgeon, regarded by many as the greatest English-speaking preacher ever to live, preached to thousands each Sunday. However, mega-churches that are openly consumer-driven tend to adopt a willingness to do whatever it takes not only to build a new customer base (i.e., create new churchgoers) but also to maintain customer loyalty (i.e., keep churchgoers coming back). In other words, this extreme involves listening to honest frustrations and then *defining the church's identity* in terms of avoiding those frustrations.

Extreme Two

The second extreme is simply not to listen to the voices of frustration at all. This extreme can take all sorts of forms. It can be as common as the regular churchgoer who shrugs off a recent defector from his church as a fact of life. ("You win a few, you lose a few.") It can be the campus ministry staff member who has consciously decided to avoid discussions about local churches in that college's area, since even the opinions within his ministry are so diverse. It can even be the pastor who has heard members' frustrations but answers them all the same: "Try to show up anyway."

The Origins of Disappointment

To avoid such extremes, we need to do some much-needed listening. Apathy and disillusionment with a local church do *not* arise from a vacuum; they have *some* origin. Why is the local church not prioritized in the lives of professing believers the way she used to be? What are people saying?

The following scenarios are representative of countless actual comments. Perhaps they have been upon the lips of close friends or family; or, perhaps, they have been upon yours.

◆ ◆ ◆

*"I stopped attending church during my college years because that's when I started understanding what the Church **really** is about. I mean, look for yourself! Look in the Book of Acts, for starters. Where are the new-member classes? Where are the services that start exactly at 11:00 AM and must be over exactly at noon? Where are the thirty-something Sunday school classes? And here's the real question: Where are the denominations? The answer is simple: They're not there.*

*"Some people misunderstand me when I say this, so I want to be clear. I do believe in the Church, with a capital 'C'. People tend to think of the 'church' as a building with a steeple where they meet for worship. **That's not it at all!** The Church is a worldwide group of people who are all brothers and sisters in Jesus Christ. They aren't connected by denominational ties or economic status or worship styles. They are a group that is connected by a living faith in Christ and by a desire to love other people, whether or not those people look like them. This Church has been around for two-thousand years and*

always will be around!

*"It was in college that I began to make the mental shift from the 'institutional' church to a 'more biblical' understanding of the Church. Ironically, this was spurred on by my trips home, during which I would find myself at the table listening to my parents talk about our church. Squabbles over buildings, nursery duty, bringing which casserole to which event . . . is **that** what the Church is supposed to look like?"*

◆ ◆ ◆

Perhaps this is the most commonly heard voice of all. It is the voice of someone who has, interestingly, taken hold of a key biblical truth. When Christians worldwide repeat the Apostles' Creed and speak of "the holy catholic church," they are confessing a truth that comes through loud and clear from the Word of God. It is this: the Church is, indeed, a worldwide phenomenon, and the Christian of the twenty-first century may truthfully speak of having brothers and sisters, not only all over the world, but down through the millennia of God's saving plan. Furthermore, we cannot deny that certain assumed practices in most churches today (Sunday schools, for example) are absent from the New Testament, as are denominations themselves.

It may very well be, though, that the international nature of the Church presents some unique challenges if you tend to believe the sort of scenario spun above. It may seem like a simplistic question, but consider this: If the Church is to be made up of people who are to exhibit and share real love, how then do you tangibly practice such love with someone ten time zones away? In other words, saying, "I am part of the worldwide body of Christ, a body that loves one another" becomes a mere *platitude* without some sort of concrete expression of it somewhere.

Where, then, will you encounter such concrete expressions of love? (Keep reading.)

Similarly, some say that the body of Christ should not be connected by denominational ties, but only by Christ Himself. Again, this—at face value—is hard to dispute. However, we must also ask a key question: *Who is Christ?* Is He God, or man, or *both?* Did He come primarily to teach a way of living socially? morally? environmentally? Did He come to save each and every individual on earth, or did He come to save a particular people?

Such questions (and there are certainly many more good ones!) begin to get at a difficulty for someone who might say, "I am simply a Christian," or, "I have no creed but Christ." The difficulty is that, all over the world, people who want only to believe in Christ understand Christ in diametrically different ways. In reality, they believe in wildly different ideas of Christ and might find it hard to sit in the same church building.

If this is the case, then we all must refine our idea of "Christ" and "Christianity," seeking to be as biblical as possible. As you do, you will likely begin to find a particular *subset* of Christendom with which you identify or relate. In other words, there are instances in which you *are* willing to define yourself in terms of like-mindedness with particular Christians. *Enter the local church.*

◆ ◆ ◆

"My church? It's the outdoors. I've always loved nature, but it wasn't until college that I actually understood from a biblical point of view why this was appropriate.

"When I reached the campus, I ended up becoming involved in a ministry that really prioritized biblical teaching. Something I heard there that I had never thought about before is that God rules over everything that He has made, and, therefore, everything that we do is to be part of worshiping Him. So often, Christians live their lives divided into two big compartments: 'sacred' and 'secular.' But that isn't what Scripture tells us. It says, 'Whether you eat or drink or whatever you do, do it all for the glory of God.'

"It suddenly hit me how relevant this was to my perception of God's presence when I was outdoors. Now I know why I've never felt closest to God in church. I don't have to be in a sanctuary on a Sunday morning to worship God—all of my life is to be worship to Him! I can worship God just as much when I'm mountain biking with friends as when I'm sitting in a pew singing a hymn. One of my favorite passages is the beginning of the nineteenth Psalm: 'The heavens declare the glory of God; the skies proclaim the work of his hands.' There are times when I'm outside lying on my back, looking up at the stars, and it does something for me that no church service has ever been able to do.

"When I get away on the weekends, I still try to make Sunday mornings a 'special' block of time by having a sort of one-man worship service. I usually read a passage of Scripture—sometimes aloud—and pray and sing to God. I

can honestly say that when I get back from trips like that, I feel refreshed down to my bones. I have no gripe with people who choose to be in church on Sunday. I just hope they go home feeling like I do."

◆ ◆ ◆

It is hard not to be envious! To be ruthlessly honest, sitting in a comfortable spot outdoors somewhere, overlooking a beautiful expanse, *does* seem to beat the prospect of sitting in a pew or chair—perhaps with tone-deaf worshipers on either side—for an hour or more. As our nature lover reminded us, the Scriptures do speak glowingly of the ability of the creation to draw our minds and hearts to the Creator.

However, there are certain things that creation is *not* able to do for our spiritual well-being. For instance, the nineteenth Psalm, mentioned above, begins on the note of how the creation evokes praise to God, but it goes on to say what *the Scriptures alone are able to do.* "The law of the LORD is perfect, reviving the soul. The statutes of the LORD are trustworthy, making wise the simple" (v. 7). Are quiet lakes and mountain trails beneficial? Of course. They cannot, however, provide us with the particulars of the good news that sinners so desperately need.

Our outdoor worshiper still expresses a laudable need to read the Bible. It is interesting, though, that, when professing believers are left to themselves, portions of the Scriptures tend to be read and reread, while other portions go neglected, if not utterly ignored. If all the Christians over the last hundred years were polled about their devotional reading, biblical books such as Zephaniah and Nahum would make a rather poor showing.

But, according to Jesus, *all* the books of what we now call the Old Testament are about His person and work (see Luke 24:27, 44). We need to hear from the whole counsel of God's Word.

If the essence of Christianity is Who Jesus is and what He did for needy sinners, and if that information is conveyed in *every* book of the Bible, then we need not only *exposure* to all of it, but even *teaching* from all of it. This is a tall order, one that the creation itself—and even individual reading alone—cannot achieve. We need to hear from those whom God has especially gifted and instructed to teach us His Word.

The fresh air will be invigorating, and the view will be enviable, but our outdoorsy friend will also *miss* certain sensory experiences by not attending a local church. Sadly, he will miss the sight of a new believer's face as baptism is received; the sound of God's character being celebrated corporately in song; the touch of a fellow believer's handshake or hug.

◆ ◆ ◆

"To be honest, I would say that, as things stand now, my campus ministry is my 'church.' My first year I suppose I did the typical freshman thing for someone from a churched background. I hit campus and began enjoying my newfound freedom, and part of that freedom involved sleeping in regularly on Sunday mornings. I can't help but feel a little bit justified, though. You have no idea how often my parents dragged all of us to church—if the doors were

open for a church activity, we were there.

*"After a while, however, I began to miss the—I don't know what to call it—
the **rhythm** of a weekly meeting with other Christians. And, honestly, my
churchless schedule left me feeling guilty, too. So one Sunday morning, I finally
dragged myself out of bed and started visiting some local churches.*

*"The problem was that—and I hate to say this—attending those churches
gave me the opportunity to see what I had been missing, and it wasn't very
pretty. Each church I attended—and I visited a cross-section of denominations—was basically the same. Everything was geared toward the folks who
were already involved. The sermons didn't connect with me or my life in
school, and no one—repeat, **no one**—invited me or my friends to eat lunch, or
paid us much attention. If I were in their shoes, I hope I would have tried a
little harder.*

*"Then a friend invited me to a campus Christian fellowship, and after a
few visits I was hooked. Now my week doesn't feel right if I miss it! Every
week the speaker seems to know exactly what I need to hear. For the first time,
I'm **excited** to hear about God's Word. And the staff and students who attend
seem really interested in reaching out to others.*

*"My campus ministry **is my congregation.** I'm sure at some point I'll
reconnect with a local church, but I feel that God understands where I am
right now."*

◆ ◆ ◆

Many a professing believer has had a similar experience. Perhaps
for those further along in life, the remedy was a weekly Bible study
or fellowship group, but the frustration was the same. The local

church was tried and—at some personal level—found wanting.

Despite that fact, here is someone who is now involved in the lives of fellow believers, hungry to learn more about God's Word, and even desiring to reach out to others. Why in the world would we want to second-guess such an individual?

There may be certain questions that are going unasked, though. For example, does this person ever have meaningful interaction with believers of other ages or economic brackets? If this individual is, say, twenty years old, how likely is it that he will be blessed by fellowship with an elderly Christian widow—someone who has lived three times longer than he has and experienced wars, the loss of a spouse, grandchildren, and decades of wrestling with the gospel? Such women are rather scarce on university campuses, and they are less likely to be found in a young mothers' or weekly office Bible study. But they are to be found—among other places—in the local church.

Also, the fellowship and good biblical teaching that this student is receiving are commendable; but what about other avenues to spiritual growth? For instance, what about the sacraments—baptism and the Lord's Supper? We underestimate the need for these in our spiritual growth. But Christians throughout the centuries have considered them indispensable for becoming godly men or women; and, not just any person can administer them. For instance, Paul had dire things to say about *inappropriately* partaking of the Lord's Supper (see 1 Cor. 11:30).

If the sacraments are to be administered uniquely by ordained clergy of local churches, as this book will contend, what will this believer do about Jesus' command to "do this in remembrance of Me"? This divine, loving command is for our spiritual development. Will this be addressed?

◆ ◆ ◆

"Actually, we attend several churches in town. Don't get me wrong—I don't mean that we attend all of them each Sunday or each week. What I mean is that after visiting around, my husband and I found different needs being met at different churches.

"The one that we primarily attend has an absolutely fantastic music ministry. The music minister seems to share our tastes. Honestly, Sunday morning worship now feels like a little slice of heaven for us.

*"On the other hand, our children desperately need a vibrant youth ministry. The church where we worship on Sunday mornings has a weak youth program. Fortunately, another church close to our house has **the** youth group in town. A lot of our children's friends attend there as well. It's exciting to see them be a part of it.*

"Another area church has great midweek Bible studies that are arranged according to age group. So, while our children are at Wednesday night youth group, we attend a home Bible study. It gives us the solid Bible teaching we know we need.

"It would be wonderful to get all this at one church, but right now this seems the best way to meet our different needs."

◆ ◆ ◆

This is a different sort of voice. This person has not neglected the local church. Instead, she has expressed an admirable willingness to go the extra mile—quite literally. Furthermore, she and her husband have realized that their *subjective* experience in worship is ultimately not enough for their spiritual well-being. There must also be *objective* truth in the form of, as she said, "solid Bible teaching."

Again, however, key questions remain. For instance, what are these parents modeling to their children about truly being a part of a body of believers, i.e., a local church? If they never become members of any one particular congregation, then the children are—probably unwittingly—being taught by example that it is acceptable to *participate* in church activities without giving back to that local church through active membership.

On the other hand, if the family *does* choose to join one of the churches—perhaps the one in which they worship on Sunday mornings—what are the children learning in regard to church membership? If the parents continue to "make the rounds" of various other church bodies, are they communicating that their membership commitment is merely a "rubber stamp"?

◆ ◆ ◆

In the early part of last century, a young Welsh preacher named Martyn Lloyd-Jones made the following statement to his small congregation:

> People complain about the dwindling congrega-
> tions and how the churches are going down. Why

are people ceasing to attend places of worship? Why is it, that last Sunday night I noticed that, while the places of worship in Cardiff were only sparsely attended, the trains coming from . . . seaside places were packed out? Why did these people spend their day at the seaside and in other places rather than in the House of God worshipping? Well, the answer is perfectly plain. They obviously prefer to be at the seaside and feel that they get more benefit there than they do in their chapels and churches. Now it is no use our arguing with people like that, it is no use our telling them that they really do not get greater benefit there, because they honestly believe that they do.[2]

Lloyd-Jones' honesty is refreshing. Present attitudes about the local church *within the Christian community* necessitate the same sort of honesty. Forget a grueling train ride to a beach somewhere. Today's professing believer can sleep to a comfortable hour on Sunday morning; brew a perfect cup of coffee; sit down in front of a monitor (still in sleeping/lounging attire); engage in cyber-chats with distant family and friends; and, then, head off to a relaxed lunch somewhere. All the while, he can congratulate himself that he understands Christianity well enough not to feel any hang-ups about not attending a local church. Cornering such an individual with the admonition that "you-ought-to-be-in-a-church-on-Sunday-if-you-value-your-soul" will probably sound something like static, and be met with a blank stare. Such individuals deserve honest, forthright feedback to their honest and forthright frustrations.

In the chapters that follow, we will speak to such frustrations by addressing a deceptively simple question: *What role* **could** *the local church play in my spiritual well being?*

We will be talking about *ecclesiology,* that is, the study of the nature and work of the Church. Do not let the term put you off. The issues and tone of this book are as relevant as your weekly planner and as important as outreach to the needy.

Chapter Two will lay the groundwork by establishing what we mean by "the Church." Most people do not think about the Church because they do not know *what* to think about the Church. Some biblical categories can help our thinking.

Chapter Three will then bring what may have sounded like abstract concepts into more concrete terms. It will examine how the Church manifests herself via the *local* church. Church "membership"–a term not used *per se* in the Scriptures–will also be considered.

Chapter Four will address this question: Given that there are so many areas where the church *could* focus her attention, where *should* she focus it? If the Bible provides a local church with a job description, what is it?

Chapter Five will consider the identity of the local church: What does it mean that God identifies with a church on earth? With whom (humanly speaking) is a church to identify?

Chapter Six will consider the authority structures that exist in the local church ("Just who's in charge here anyway?"). If the Bible is the ultimate authority for a church, what does that look like in practice? Furthermore, what do the officers of a church have to do with the people in the seats, and *vice versa?*

Chapter Seven will paint a picture of a local church as a body of people that love. It sounds like a platitude, but it involves real, tangible activities. What are they?

Finally, we will conclude in Chapter Eight by discussing the future of God's Church, both in the short run and in her ultimate, long-term destiny.

Are you frustrated with the local church? You may be in good company, and it may be that you are asking just the right questions.

2

The Idea of the Church

"You cannot have God for your Father unless you have the church for your Mother."

~Cyprian

"But as it is now our purpose to discourse of the visible Church, let us learn, for her single title of Mother, how useful, nay, how necessary the knowledge of her is, since there is no other means of entering into life unless she conceive us in the womb and give us birth, unless she nourish us at her breasts, and, in short, keep us under her charge and government, until, divested of mortal flesh, we become like the angels. . . . Moreover, beyond the pale of the Church no forgiveness of sins, no salvation, can be hoped for."

~John Calvin

Two open cans of paint sit at my feet. The label on the first can reads "Country Heather Green," the other "Cornsilk Yellow."

"So," my wife asks me, "which color do you think will go best in our bedroom?"

The question is innocent enough, and yet I can feel my brow furrowing. Anxiety grows. "Uh, I don't know . . ." I say weakly, "Which one do you like?"

Mercifully, my wife delivers her best "Thanks-a-Bundle" look and dismisses me.

My problem is not apathy. The bedroom needs a paint job. It is the *question* that stumps me. My mind races to connect to something–anything that will shed some light on the "best" color for our walls. The blank looks that my wife incurs betray the fact that I am lost in the world of color palettes and fabric swatches. I do not know what to think, so I simply do not think anything.

◆ ◆ ◆

Most Christians spend about as much time thinking about the Church as I do about the color of my bedroom. Could the reason be simply a lack of categories?

Perhaps the reason is this: *most of us do not think about the Church because we do not know how to think about the Church.*

Just as I was clueless as to how to think about what color would go best on which walls in my house, so also the average Christian today often does not have a clue about the Church. Our predicament is the same: We do not know what to think, so too often we simply do not *carefully* think anything.

Our thinking goes something like this: *Ummm, yeah, the Church– that's good. I'm all for the church. Your church sounds good and my church sounds good. Oh, whatever–who's to say what a church should be and which church is best?*

Today's Church (and here we are speaking in the sense of all the people everywhere who constitute it) is like an insecure teenager. A teen struggling with self-image has no idea *who he or she is* and ends up morphing into a different person with each passing crowd, becoming like whoever happens to be closest at the time.

The Church today is undergoing a similar identity crisis. Without a clear "self-image," a constant morphing of church (and parachurch) models results, until what is left is an amorphous blob. The Church today has lost a sense of its constituting idea—the idea that defines who she is; the idea defining how she works; the idea describing her origins; etc.

Fortunately, our God suffers from no such lack of clarity! On the contrary, the "Church" began and continues to exist as God's idea. What we are saying is that—in this fast-paced, information-glutted new millennium—the members who constitute God's Church on earth have lost sight of their Founding Father's original idea.

◆ ◆ ◆

Without a sense of self-identity that draws from God's idea of the Church, we are left without categories. Without categories, local churches simply take on the characteristics of whoever happens to be closest at that time. Paul anticipated this temptation in the Ephesian believers and exhorted them:

> Prepare God's people for works of service, so
> that the body of Christ may be built up until we all
> reach unity in the faith and in the knowledge of the
> Son of God and become mature, attaining to the

> whole measure of the fullness of Christ. Then we
> will no longer be infants, tossed back and forth by
> the waves, and blown here and there by every wind
> of teaching and by the cunning and craftiness of
> men in their deceitful scheming. (4:12–14)

Just as a sixteen-year-old will never learn to grow and appreciate his life until he decides who he is, so the Church must learn to see herself through God's eyes. *He* must define her. The Church must learn to think God's thoughts after Him about her own identity. She must glean her categories from Him and what He thinks about her.

At the same time, she must also learn *what she is not.* She must reject unnecessary baggage that is not part of her God-given character. Otherwise, says Paul, she will continue to be the hapless victim of the latest religious whim.

God has graciously given us some wonderful concrete word pictures that help express His idea of the Church. He calls the Church: (1) A Building, (2) A Body, and (3) A Bride. By unpacking the richness of these three word pictures—or object lessons—we will come closer to understanding God's own overarching idea for His Church.

A Building

First, Paul uses the image of a **building** to describe the Church.

> Consequently, you are no longer foreigners and
> aliens, but fellow citizens with God's people and

members of God's household, built on the foundation of the apostles and prophets, with Christ Jesus
himself as the chief cornerstone. In him the whole
building is joined together and rises to become a
holy temple in the Lord. And in him you too are
being built together to become a dwelling in which
God lives by his Spirit. (Eph. 2:19–22)

The people of God are like a building. Notice that the passage
does not say that the people of God *dwell in a building* or that the people of God *are primarily supposed to live out their existence in a building,*
but that the people of God *are* a building.

Wayne Mack and David Swavely, in their book on the Church
entitled *Life in the Father's House,* recall the time when as children they
would get caught running through the church building and climbing
on pews. Soon, inevitably, the crotchety, old deacon would bark at
them, "Get off there, don't you know this is God's house? You can't
do that in here."

Granted, any place of worship ought to be treated with respect
and given special care. But this can create misunderstanding. Church
buildings, *per se,* do not possess an inherent sacredness. It is the building *inside* of the building to which the Bible refers. The stones that
create her are flesh and blood. It is a temple, Paul says, that has been
made holy by Christ, the chief cornerstone.

The temple mount in the life of any Jewish Christian of Paul's day
would have had an ocean of nostalgia attached to it. When a Jew

stood before the temple of God, he stood in a place where God lived—and not in a mere spiritual sense, but in a visible and audible expression of His majesty. If you were a Jew then, you would have been told from the time that you could understand anything about how God had met Moses "over the mercy seat" of the ark of the covenant, and how, during the dedication of the Tabernacle, God came down in a great ball of fire, the Shekinah glory, to meet and speak with His people in a visible way.

The temple represented another pinnacle in the life of Israel, reached under Solomon. King Solomon spent exorbitant amounts of money and energy building what had to be one of the most magnificent edifices of the ancient world. Upon the dedication of this temple, the Presence of God again descended and filled the temple with smoke so that the priests could not perform their functions (1 Kings 8).

The point is this: the temple was the locus of the very Presence of God. But do not miss the image. Paul is saying that this same Presence now dwells *in the Church*. Jeremiah 3:16–17, speaking about the Ark of the Covenant, says:

> In those days, . . . men will no longer say, 'The ark of the covenant of the LORD.' It will never enter their minds or be remembered; it will not be missed, nor will another one be made. At that time they will call Jerusalem the Throne of the LORD.

This prophecy is astounding. God will make His home in the

hearts and minds of His people. It is no coincidence that, in Acts 2:3, Luke describes what looked like "tongues of fire" resting on the heads of those who were there. The Holy Spirit of God had arrived. The Shekinah had returned, not over an ark, but in the hearts of His people!

There is much talk in evangelicalism today about rebuilding the Temple in Jerusalem in hopes that this will usher in the second coming of Christ. But what purpose would that serve? Why would God regress to return to a physical locale when He has already so powerfully manifested His Presence in the hearts of His people? *The temple mount is the Church, gathering together and worshiping, Sunday after Sunday.* The value of *that* building infinitely outweighs the value of the Old Testament temple or any temple that some think will someday soon be built. The *Church* is God's temple now!

The implications of Paul's words are overwhelming. This is not the only place where Paul uses this kind of language. First Timothy 3:14–15 borrows the metaphor and extends it:

> Although I hope to come to you soon, I am writing you these instructions so that, if I am delayed, you will know how people ought to conduct themselves in God's household, which is the church of the living God, the pillar and foundation of the truth.

The Church, Paul says, is the "pillar and foundation" of truth. The Church, then, is the support and protection of the very truth of God.

Truth, in the world and in the lives of believers, has no stability if it does not have the Church. The Church is the support system of Truth itself. There can be no higher calling.

What does this mean? To state it simply: If anyone ever hopes to "find God" or to "discover truth," it will never happen securely outside of the ministry of the Church.

I work with college students, and I cannot count the number of students who have decided to take a semester off from school to "find themselves." "I just want to know what's real, you know? I need to find God." But if it is God you seek, do not waste your time looking for Him in a place where He did not promise to be. Only in the Church can we find the fullness of truth, make sense of our lives, and meet our deepest longings.

To push the point further, without the Church you cannot understand the Bible. God has commissioned the Church (not seminaries, not theologians, not well-intentioned institutions) to be the caretaker of His truth found in the Word—so much that to attempt to understand the Bible without the oversight and influence of the Church is an exercise in futility.

This might upset some. Some might protest: "What you are teaching denies a fundamental doctrine of the Reformation. The doctrine of the priesthood of all believers says that every Christian has the right to interpret the Bible in his or her own way."

Actually, this is *not* what the doctrine of the priesthood of all believers says.

The Reformers stressed that each person is directly connected to God through Christ the Mediator. We need no *earthly, institutional mediator* between God and us in order to maintain our relationship to Him. No earthly priest or designate is needed to grant us forgiveness of sin. But it was never the intention of the Reformers to say that, therefore, anyone was free to imagine any interpretation of the Bible that he wanted.

Commenting on the Reformers' understanding of the concept of *sola Scriptura* ("the Scriptures alone"), Michael Scott Horton says, "Of course, the laity were not to use the Bible as a wax nose to be shaped by private, subjective opinion, which *Sola Scriptura* has come to mean in some circles today; rather, it meant that all believers had the right and responsibility to read, understand, and obey God's Word—*with* the rest of the Church (though certainly not without it)."[1]

No one is given the right to interpret the Bible in any way in which he or she pleases. It is only in the context of the corporate body of believers that the truth of the Bible can be adequately understood and applied.

Peter Leithart has written a delightful collection of fairy tales entitled *Wise Words*. In one story, "The Monster's House," Leithart tells of a man named Zeke who goes in search of his family, which had recently disappeared. He suspects that they have been taken captive by the legendary "monster" that lives in a castle on top of a smoked-veiled hill. As Zeke approaches the fortress, it is not like any building he has ever seen:

> The house was made of pure white brick, but the bricks were like nothing Zeke had ever seen. They were of irregular size and shape, so that Zeke,

though he knew something about buildings, could not understand how the house held together. It teetered back and forth, threatening each moment to collapse into a heap. Yet, supported by some unseen power, it never fell.

More strangely than this, it seemed to Zeke that each brick of the house was in constant motion. At first, he was certain the morning light and the misty clouds were playing tricks with his eyes. The more he looked, the more convinced Zeke became that each brick was alive and breathing![2]

Zeke soon finds that his family is not lost at all. They have come to the monster's house on their own, as if drawn by some unseen delight. Later, Zeke meets the "monster," only to find that he is no monster at all. Rather, he was the wisest, kindest man he has ever met. The story ends with Zeke and his family being transformed into living stones and taking their own place in the great castle.

The story makes for great fantasy and is not bad theology, either. If we are living stones, then we are a part of what God is building for Himself. Other "stones" are packed in around us. They are uncomfortable. They stick their noses into our business. They get involved in our lives more than we might like. They are often too close. They push and contort us into positions we do not like. They sin against us and we sin against them. They force us into uninvited molds. It can be tempting to think of such an edifice as a "monster's house."

Yet, when seen through the eye of the Master Architect, the whole building rises as a glorious edifice, a dwelling place for His Presence. Far from being a prison, life in this house brings true freedom.

This house is the Church.

A Body

Second, Paul uses the image of a ***body***. Ephesians 4:3–6 says this:

> Make every effort to keep the unity of the Spirit through the bond of peace. There is one body and one Spirit—just as you were called to one hope when you were called—one Lord, one faith, one baptism; one God and Father of all, who is over all and through all and in all.

Paul says that, if the idea of the Church is to be grasped, she must be seen as a body.

At first glance, this might seem naïve. Paul says that there is an essential unity that exists for those who call themselves Christians. How dare those who talk about the Church mention the word *unity?*

We must face it: in our day, the Church of the Lord Jesus can be called many things, but "unified" is not one of them. Denominations seem to multiply exponentially with every passing decade. A recent statistic reported that Protestant denominations number approximately 20,000! That's denominations, not churches! Talk of unity among Christians today sounds almost blindly unrealistic.

Perhaps more than ever, the Church needs to hear Paul's words. His appeal to the Ephesian believers for unity is not based upon overly optimistic, wishful thinking. He centers his appeal on the very character of God. Since Christ is one, since the Spirit is one, and since the Trinity is one essence, the visible expression of Christ's body, the Church, *must* be one as well. "Is Christ divided?" he asks to the Church in Corinth.[3] No, there is "one body and one Spirit . . . one Lord . . . one God and Father of all."[4]

Consider also Jesus' passionate appeal for the unity of the Church in His High Priestly Prayer in John 17:20b-21, 23. There He prays "for those who will believe in me through their message, that all of them may be one, Father, just as you are in me and I am in you . . . May they be brought to complete unity to let the world know that you sent me."

John Murray, systematic theologian from Westminster Seminary, noted that John 17:21 must not be divorced from John 17:20. Murray said: "To disassociate the unity for which Jesus prayed from all that is involved in believing on him is to rend asunder what our Lord joined together. And this believing on Him is not a faith that can be abstracted from the total witness of the New Testament to the identity of Jesus."[5] In other words, there can be no real unity if there is no unity around the truth of who Jesus is.

Therefore, any kind of thinking that tries to impose an arbitrary unity upon members of the Church must be rejected. Jesus and Paul are not arguing for "unity for unity's sake." "Can't we all just get along?" is not enough to create the kind of close communion that our Lord desires. Unity must always be a unity of *truth* in the Scripture.

But second, Jesus' and Paul's words about unity must be taken with grave seriousness. Christians must own up to the fact that the lack of apparent unity among the churches that profess the Christian faith in its purity is a clear violation of what Jesus and Paul are saying.

Does the Church long to be one? Does she work for its peace and purity? Is she willing to sacrifice pride and unbiblical distinctions in our fellowship for the oneness of the visible body of Christ? Sinful complacency regarding the unity of the Church must be rebuked as an evil that is dishonoring to Christ.

Scriptural teaching on the unity of the body creates many practical considerations. For instance, when someone is converted, he is no longer primarily from New York or California or wherever. He is no longer primarily male or female. He is no longer primarily African American or Hispanic or white. He is no longer primarily upper class or upper middle class or lower class. A Christian is primarily a member of the *ultimate body,* the body of Christ.

How flippantly Christians speak about the manner in which they choose with whom they will and will not associate. "Mind you," they say, "I am not prejudiced or anything. I just don't like the same music that they like. We just come from different cultural backgrounds." But is this not a bold-faced admission that musical tastes and cultural backgrounds are *more* fundamental to their self-understanding than the fact that they are redeemed in Christ? The lifeblood that is pumping through this body is the person and work of Jesus Christ. If

He is one, we must be one as well.

The image of the body that speaks to the Church about its unity time speaks to its diversity as well. Paul deals with the early Corinthian church with consummate wisdom as he talks about the varied giftedness of those in the body. Different and varied gifts are given, but none are more important than the others. Paul explains in 1 Corinthians 12:14, 18–19: "Now the body is not made up of one part but many. . . . But in fact God has arranged the parts in the body, every one of them, just as he wanted them to be. If they were all one part, where would the body be?"

Of all the issues facing the Church today, the unity of the body certainly is one of the most practical and frustrating. Sin creates self-absorption so that believers are unable to appreciate the fact that God's plan of salvation for His people is bigger than they are. Only the total body of Christ with all its glorious differences is up to the challenge of taking the gospel to all peoples and all nations.

Unity, therefore, is not opposed to diversity in God's economy. Choosing between one or the other is not necessary. Both are perfectly realized in the new self-definition that comes from those who are members of this body known as the Church.

But how quickly we forget! How many churches have been torn to pieces over the most mundane controversies? How many congregations have split over a building campaign? How much gossip about a church's present leadership has ravaged relationships and sent unity packing?

At the very least, the unity of the body of Christ obligates (forces!)

the believers within her walls to make a conscious effort to learn to practice something that never came naturally to any sinner: submission.

Submission, ultimately, to Christ means that I put His concerns over my own when I am in the church.

Submission means that I repent of what I so glibly refer to as "constructive criticism" and call it what it is: gossip.

Submission means that I accept the fact that no church will ever do everything to my tastes, and the sooner I stop expecting it to do so, the better.

The Church is a body, and I am either a productive member of that organism or I am actively contributing to its dismemberment.

A Bride

Finally, the Bible describes the Church as a *bride.*

In chapter five of Ephesians, Paul draws a direct parallel between earthly marriages and the ultimate marriage, that of Christ to His Church:

> Husbands, love your wives, just as Christ loved the church and gave himself up for her to make her holy, cleansing her by the washing with water through the word, and to present her to himself as a radiant church, without stain or wrinkle or any other blemish, but holy and blameless. In this same way, husbands ought to love their wives as their own bodies. He who loves his wife loves himself.

After all, no one ever hated his own body, but he feeds and cares for it, just as Christ does the church—for we are members of his body. "For this reason a man will leave his father and mother and be united to his wife, and the two will become one flesh." This is a profound mystery—but I am talking about Christ and the church. However, each one of you also must love his wife as he loves himself, and the wife must respect her husband.[6]

This kind of language appears throughout the pages of Scripture. Isaiah 62:5 says, "As a young man marries a maiden, so will your sons marry you; as a bridegroom rejoices over his bride, so will your God rejoice over you."

Paul gets most graphic in 2 Corinthians 11:2 when he says, "I am jealous for you with a godly jealousy. I promised you to one husband, to Christ, so that I might present you as a pure virgin to him."

At the end of time, says Revelation 19, all of human history will *culminate* with the Marriage Supper of the Lamb when Christ takes His Bride: "Let us rejoice and be glad and give him glory! For the wedding of the Lamb has come, and his bride has made herself ready."[7]

The Bible is clear. Jesus has honeymoon affections for His Bride. Even in the midst of our sinful ugliness, this delight for His people is evident. Before the urgency of wedding photographers came along, it was tradition that the bride and groom would not see each other on the day of the wedding. But our bridegroom not only stays with us throughout our "engagement," He is also responsible for creating the beauty that adorns us. The Ephesians 5 passage says that Jesus worked salvation for the Church, ". . . to make her holy, cleansing her by the washing with water through the word, and to present her to himself as a radiant church, without stain or wrinkle or any other blemish, but holy and blameless."

Performing weddings is undoubtedly one of the greatest privileges of my ministry. I have the best seat in the house. The groom and the best man enter first and stand at the end of a long aisle waiting for the bride to come down in all her beauty. However, my wife has encouraged me to notice another glorious feature of weddings, the groom's reaction. She says that you can tell a lot about the future of a marriage by the groom's reaction to his bride. When doors swing open and the music begins, if the groom yawns, questionable husband. However, if he is absolutely enthralled and stands on the verge of tears as his beloved comes toward him—imagine their future.

One time, a groom moved me to tears with his reaction. On this occasion, the organist, who had a flare for the dramatic, opened up with an absolutely regal version of "Crown Him with Many Crowns." As the doors opened and the bride came into view, smiling from ear to ear, the young man's knees buckled. His jaw dropped open and big, frightened, smiling tears ran down his red face. He almost did not make it through the service, so enamored was he with his bride.

Christians typically think that the moral of this story goes something like this: "So we need to love Jesus just as this young man loved his bride. We need to have the same affection for Him that grooms have for their future wives during a wedding. Let's pray." But that would reverse the image and miss the point. On the contrary, the Ephesians passage says that *Christ* is the bridegroom and we, the Church, are the one coming down the aisle.

The point is this: when we begin in our hearts to look down the aisle of our own salvation and see Christ, standing there with anticipation, knees buckling under the weight of the beauty that He has created and sustained, with tears flowing for the delight that He takes in us—only then will we begin to be the Church that God designed for His Son, the groom. Only then will we find the courage to sacrifice for the Church in the way in which we are called to sacrifice. Only then will we find the patience to put up with each other with grace and forgiveness. Only then will we find the humility to accept into our fellowship the poor, the hurting, the downtrodden, and the broken.

As James "Bebo" Elkin, Area Coordinator for Reformed University Ministries, alludes: "If Jesus loved the Church enough to die for it, then we can love it enough to be patient with it." How true.

3

The Visibility of the Church

"Some keep the Sabbath going to church; I keep it staying at home, With a bobolink for a chorister, and an orchard for a dome."[1]

~Emily Dickinson

"Jesus went to Nazareth, where he had been brought up, and on the Sabbath day he went into the synagogue, as was his custom."

~The Gospel of Luke

Perhaps the most ingenious means of recruitment that the U.S. Navy ever devised was during the mid-1980s. When the movie *Top Gun* was showing in theaters nationwide, the Navy had the presence of mind to set up recruitment tables in the lobbies of some of those same theaters. After having just seen the adventures of a naval pilot played by Tom Cruise, having just been in the pilot's seat of an F-14, and having just seen the U.S. Navy come out on top against the Soviets, moviegoers exited the screen room to find naval recruiters on standby. No doubt, such tactics were effective.

Now, we would not want to presuppose any dishonesty on the part of those who operated these recruitment tables. However, we can only imagine the response of the young man who, under the influence of *Top Gun*–induced excitement about the thought of being in the Navy, signed up for it, only to find that it involved very real discipline, early mornings, menial chores, and colleagues from all walks of life. The abstraction seemed so wonderful; the reality was a bit more trying. And where in the world was Kelly McGillis?

Talking about the Church can induce similar responses.

As long as we are talking about the beautiful metaphors of Chapter Two, truths about the Church at-large, it is easy to proclaim: "Count me in."

Then, we walk into the church down the street, with all its bickering, messiness, and odd people, and the enthusiasm quickly dies down. In fact, it may evaporate.

In his book *The Kingdom and the Power,* Peter J. Leithart describes this mindset well:

> Some Christians are rather like a man going through mid-life crisis who dreams of a perfect woman to replace his aging wife; the concept of a perfect "invisible" church is used to rationalize abandonment of what is, to all appearances, a sagging, wrinkled, "visible" church.
>
> Nowhere, to be sure, do the New Testament writers flinch from a full acknowledgment of sin and turmoil within the church. The apostles would have no doubt grimly nodded if told of some wit's sug-

gestion that the church is like Noah's ark: if it weren't for the rain outside, you couldn't stand the stench inside.[2]

Leithart makes use of terminology that is important for us to understand: the Church as both "invisible" and "visible." We must learn the distinction if we are to love Christ's bride.

What do we mean by these two terms?

The *Westminster Confession of Faith,* a doctrinal treatise drawn up by a group of ministers (or "divines," as they were called) in the 1640s, provides the following definitions:

> The catholic or universal church, which is invisible, consists of the whole number of the elect, that have been, are, or shall be gathered into one, under Christ the head thereof; and is the spouse, the body, the fullness of him that filleth all in all.
>
> The visible church, which is also catholic or universal under the gospel (not confined to one nation as before under the law), consists of all those throughout the world that profess the true religion, together with their children; and is the kingdom of the Lord Jesus Christ, the house and family of God, out of which there is no ordinary possibility of salvation.[3]

The Invisible Church: This is the "holy catholic church" of the

Apostles' Creed; it is the totality of all the people that ever have been, are, or will be truly saved by grace through the blood of Jesus Christ. Only God in His infinite knowledge comprehends the invisible Church. No human being could ever fathom it, this side of heaven.

The Visible Church: This is all who profess (*profess* is a key word) to believe that they are saved by grace through the blood of Jesus Christ, as well as the children of those who make this profession. Some in this body may actually not be saved but they do profess faith. They sit in a church pew, or even on a local church committee. More important, the visible church—containing both actual believers and some who are only presumptuous in their faith—can be seen. Every local church is a part of the whole, which is the visible church.

As some have said, the invisible Church is the Church from God's perspective; the visible Church is the present-day Church from our perspective. Though these exact two terms are not present in the Bible (as is the case with other terms such as *Trinity* and *Christianity*), the concepts are.

For instance, in the Book of Romans, Paul makes a distinction between outward, professing Jews and real, inward Jews. He writes, "A man is not a Jew if he is only one outwardly, nor is circumcision merely outward and physical. No, a man is a Jew if he is one inwardly; and circumcision is circumcision of the heart, by the Spirit, not by the written code" (Rom. 2:28–29a).

Paul was drawing from Christianity's Jewish roots to help Christians understand the Church. Before Christ came, says Paul, a man could join the Old Testament Church—the people of Israel—by being physically circumcised. People from different races and religions converted to Judaism, and received the outward sign of circumcision. These converts were then entitled to participate in the life of the Jewish church, to worship in a local synagogue, and to reap all the external benefits of conversion.

However, only God knew which of these converts actually had, in receiving circumcision outwardly, been given true faith in the God of the Jews. The same was true for native-born Israelites: their circumcision on the eighth day of life was a sign that they were entitled to all the privileges of life as an "outward" or visible Jew. But each Israelite was required by God to display the fruit of an inward, invisible faith in God. Some did; some did not.

The *true* Israel, as God defined it, was made up of those who had undergone a supernatural circumcision, that is, a circumcision (or cleansing) of the heart. In other words, some were outwardly Israelites (or visible Israel), though not *heart* Israelites (or invisible Israel).

Paul echoes this same thought later when he states: "For not all who are descended from Israel are Israel. Nor because they are his descendants are they all Abraham's children" (Rom. 9:6b–7a).

Do these same distinctions hold true in the New Testament era? Consider this example. John wrote of "antichrists" who had actually emerged from within the visible community of professing believers. "They went out from us, but they did not really belong to us. For if they had belonged to us, they would have remained with us; but their going showed that none of them belonged to us" (1 John 2:19).

In other words, even in the earliest period of the New Testament

Church, there were those who *appeared* to be believers (and would have undergone Christian baptism and attended Christian worship, etc.), but who actually had not been cleansed inwardly. They were members of the visible church, but not of the invisible.

The main point, therefore, is this: *The invisible Church presently manifests herself in visible congregations of professing believers.*

But establishing this point may not necessarily change the way we think about the local church. What implications does the visibility of the church hold for us? Do we have to attend a local church regularly? For that matter, do we have to join one?

Visible Membership

Face it. No biblical passages exist that indicate actual church membership, although early church documents reveal membership soon became a regular and rigorous process.

Still, as we read through the Book of Acts and the letters to different churches, we do not find overt, how-to instructions for "Inquirers' Classes" or assimilation of new members. We also do not come across an explicit command that states: "Thou shalt be in church every Sunday." Therefore, it is fair to ask some honest questions: What justifies the practice of having "members" of a local church? Why is it not enough simply to be a member of *the* Church at-large, the body of Christ? Can't I just be a Christian? On a similar note, what rationale exists for believers attending a local church on Sunday?

For some, these are obvious questions; for others, local church membership and involvement are such established assumptions that they may never have thought to ask such questions. Whatever the case, if we are to be biblical in our thoughts and practices, we need to address these questions from the Scriptures. To do so, we must consider two types of passages: those which *explicitly* speak to church involvement, and those which *implicitly* speak to church membership.

The "custom" of Jesus

Luke 4:16 says: "He [Jesus] went to Nazareth, where he had been brought up, and on the Sabbath day he went into the synagogue, *as was his custom.*"[4]

This passage is pregnant with consequences.

First, Jesus had an established weekly routine of attending synagogue (the Jewish equivalent of the local church) on the Sabbath day. Apparently, among His hometown folk, this was known to be "his custom." If it was the Sabbath, Jesus could be found in the synagogue at worship with His fellow Jews.

Second, imagine Jesus—the Second Person of the Trinity—sitting or standing with the other worshipers, listening to a leader comment upon a text from the Scriptures, and knowing that the leader had utterly misrepresented the passage. Why would He know this? He, as God Himself, had *inspired* the passage!

Peter reminds us that the One who was at work in the writers of Scripture was "the Spirit of Christ" (1 Peter. 1:11). If a leader made a mistake in his explanation of a passage, the Author was physically present in the congregation. Yet, though such mistakes must have been made as Jesus attended His church, He, the Author, persisted in His involvement—every week.

Imagine another scene: those gathered at the synagogue are singing from a psalm, many of which are called "messianic psalms" because of their explicit references to the person and work of the coming Messiah. Imagine Jesus looking around during the psalm singing. One man's lips are not even moving. Another man's body language indicates he wishes that the whole thing would quickly end. Meanwhile, the *Object of their worship was in their very midst!*

Then another psalm is sung—this one is about Jesus' Father. Again, some sing robustly, but others are clearly half-hearted. Imagine Jesus' inward response as He beheld such apathy toward His Father. Did this paltry, sin-marred worship prompt Jesus to abandon the practice of weekly synagogue worship? On the contrary, it was "his custom."

The "habit" of early believers

Now, consider Hebrews 10:25, which reads: "Let us not give up meeting together, as some are in the habit of doing, but let us encourage one another—and all the more as you see the Day approaching."

The words "meeting together" are actually a translation of a single Greek word, *episynagoge*. Whether or not you have any familiarity with Greek, it is not difficult to recognize how much this word looks like *synagogue*. The fact that the two words appear to be similar proves nothing, though. What does this word mean?

In his commentary on the Book of Hebrews, Philip E. Hughes

provides an extensive treatment on the meaning of this particular Greek word, and he comes to this interesting conclusion: "Here . . . the term *episynagoge* should be understood as simply the regular gathering together of Christian believers for worship and exhortation in a particular place—a practice that at first took place daily (Acts 2:46), but subsequently weekly, on the first day of the week (Acts 20:7; 1 Cor. 16:2)."[5]

Apparently, the writer of Hebrews had something particular in mind when he exhorted professing Christians to keep the "habit" of "meeting together." He was recommending regular assembly on the Sabbath day for worship.

In summary: Is there a passage that plainly states, "Go to church every Sunday"? No.

But for Jesus, regular attendance at the local synagogue was "his custom." For the writer of Hebrews, such weekly meetings of worship were a "habit" that his readers were to embrace.

Should we think any differently?

Membership leads to good followers and leaders

Do the Scriptures recommend church membership?

Several passages indicate some sort of official identification with a body of believers in order for the passages to be applied. Simply put, there are certain passages of Scripture that can hardly be put into practice without such a thing as local church membership. Let us consider two types.

1. Instructions to church leaders. In a local church, there are two types of officers: elders (or overseers) and deacons. In the New Testament, particular instructions are provided for both types of officers. For our purposes, consider some of the instructions provided for elders. Here is one significant passage:

> To the elders among you, I appeal as a fellow elder, a witness of Christ's sufferings and one who also will share in the glory to be revealed: Be shepherds of God's flock that is under your care, serving as overseers—not because you must, but because you are willing, as God wants you to be; not greedy for money, but eager to serve; not lording it over those entrusted to you, but being examples to the flock (1 Pet. 5:1-3).

Paul uses the same sort of language as he bids good-bye to the elders of the church in Ephesus. He exhorts them: "Keep watch over yourselves and all the flock of which the Holy Spirit has made you overseers. Be shepherds of the church of God, which he bought with his own blood" (Acts 20:28).

Several common themes emerge from these passages.

First, the church ultimately belongs to God—it is "God's flock," "the church of God."

Second, the elders are to "be shepherds" of God's people, "not lording . . . but being examples to the flock."

Third, this flock is made up of "those entrusted to" the elders. As

Paul reminds them, the elders are not self-appointed leaders; they are leading "the flock of which *the Holy Spirit* has made you overseers."[6]

Here is the key question: If the elders are commanded to shepherd the flock, *which particular sheep make up this particular flock?* Is it every individual that ever visits that group of believers? Is it every believer in that particular city or area? Could it be every believer everywhere?

Clearly, some parameters have to be set for what we mean by this particular "flock." Church membership becomes a feasible means for elders to identify the particular sheep under their oversight.

2. Instructions to church participants. The passages above address the shepherds, but there are also passages that speak to the sheep. For instance, Hebrews 13:17 provides the following directive: "Obey your leaders and submit to their authority. They keep watch over you as men who must give an account. Obey them so that their work will be a joy, not a burden, for that would be of no advantage to you."

This simply underscores that a very real commitment—call it membership or identification or active participation—in a local church was being made by early believers. This commitment was so real that it was natural for the writer of Hebrews to command these local church folk to obey the local church leaders.

Church membership, then, provides a means for leaders to know whom they are overseeing, and it allows members to know *to whom they should submit obediently.*

Consider another example. In the Book of James, we are given directions for what to do in the case of severe sickness. "Is any one of you sick? He should call the elders of the church to pray over him and anoint him with oil in the name of the Lord" (5:14). But if you were in this situation, which particular elders would you call? Again, church membership provides a means whereby we know who "our" elders are in such a scenario.

If this is an accurate picture of what Scripture teaches, we should pause before we go any further. This bears directly upon professing Christian college students who, upon moving to school, begin to examine churches in their area. Such an examination is fine, but should this "quest" still be under way two or three years later?

Sadly, this is often the case. Believers in college—or believers whose job requires constant moves—can perceive themselves as operating in a special "zone" that frees them from the necessity of church membership. Or, perhaps, they insist on maintaining a membership only at their church back home.

But this practically nullifies receiving shepherding from officers to whom God has entrusted their spiritual oversight.

Consider this scenario: If a college-aged student from a church hundreds of miles away begins to embrace heretical views about God or salvation while at school, who will lovingly be responsible for the restoration of this student? Or if a professed Christian living and working in another city shocks family and friends by moving in with a boyfriend or girlfriend, who will love this person enough to knock on the door and ask the awkward questions that must be asked?

Suddenly, the implications of church membership are not an abstraction.

Nor are they an abstraction for those further along in life. For instance, in the scenario described above, what if the *parents* of this student know the situation but are unwilling to confront it (even, perhaps, as they are financing the student's ability to remain in school)? Who will love both the parents and the student enough to deal with the issue?

Consider yet another example. Suppose a member of a church simply ceases attending worship—not just for weeks, but for months. Surely this disappearance from church is not without reason. But who is officially responsible to notice such a thing? The elders of the church are, because they have been entrusted by God to oversee the spiritual well-being of this precious sheep.

However, we would be lopsided in our consideration if all the benefits of church membership were linked to moral or theological crises. What do the Scriptures have to say about the benefits of simply being together?

Visible Mutuality

Undoubtedly, a hallmark of American culture is individualism. In his classic account of his impressions of early America, French nobleman Alexis de Tocqueville defined individualism as "a mature and calm feeling, which disposes each member of the community to sever himself from the mass of his fellows, and to draw apart with his family and friends; so that, after he has thus formed a little circle of his own, he willingly leaves society at large to itself."[7]

In other words, to think individualistically is to think of yourself as *independent* of others, calling the shots concerning with whom you will spend time or be committed, and with whom you will not. It is not without foundation that one of the great American icons is the cowboy, alone with his thoughts, and master of all he surveys.

Not surprisingly, such Lone Rangerism has flavored the experience of American Christianity. Rather than understanding themselves in terms of the biblical metaphors used for the people of God (i.e., "I am one of the living stones in God's house," "I am one of the many parts of Christ's body"), American believers are prone to adopt a just-me-and-God mentality.

A particularly striking example of this mindset was observed one day while meeting with a college student. In this student's (commendable) attempt to read the Bible as a personal message from God for his good, the student had systematically worked through several New Testament books and *struck through all the plural pronouns,* replacing them with first person singular ones. In doing so, he had actually canonized a view of Christianity in which the object of Christ's eternal love was not a people, but rather an individual.

Such thinking did not begin in America, as church historian Richard Lovelace has noted. In describing patterns that began in the medieval period, he provides this perceptive assessment of individualism among believers, as well as the biblical response.

> The pattern of congregational life established by
> the beginning of the Middle Ages . . . has resulted
> in an individualistic spirituality that the church has
> never quite abandoned. In this model of the

Christian life the individual believer is connected to the source of grace like a diver who draws his air supply from the surface through a hose. He is essentially a self-contained system cut off from the other divers working around him. If their air supply is cut off, this does not damage him nor can he share with them the air that he receives. The situation would be no different if he were working alone a hundred miles away.

The organic metaphor for the church used by Paul absolutely negates this conception by asserting that grace is conveyed through the body of Christ along horizontal channels as well as through the vertical relationship of each believer to God. No individual, congregation or denomination of Christians is spiritually independent of the others: "The eye cannot say to the hand, 'I have no need of you,' nor again the head to the feet, 'I have no need of you'" (1 Cor. 12:21). Therefore "the normal Christian life" is not simply a function of an individual believer's relationship to God. If he is isolated from Christians around him who are designed to be part of the system through which he receives grace, or if those Christians are themselves spiritually weak, he cannot be as strong and as filled with the

Spirit as he otherwise would be.[8]

Is this too strong an assertion? After all, does not the Bible clearly teach that, ultimately, all we need is Christ? Yes, but it also teaches that *an essential means by which Christ blesses a believer is through the lives of that believer's brothers and sisters.*

In the fourth chapter of Ephesians, Paul clearly acknowledges that the blessings that come to the Body of Christ are from the Head, that is, Christ Himself. However, he also describes the process by which Christ accomplishes these blessings: "From him the whole body, joined and held together by *every supporting ligament,* grows and builds itself up in love, as *each part* does its work" (v. 16).[9] We need to catch the significance of what God's Word is teaching here. Though all capacity to grow and thrive ultimately comes from Jesus Christ, the Body experiences this development through the involvement of "every supporting ligament" and "each part." Quite simply, this means that there are no insignificant people in the local church. Each one is a means through whom the Lord blesses not only *that* church, but also *the entire* Body of Christ. It is so radical a thought that we would be hesitant to assert it, were it not clearly taught in God's Word!

In light of this truth, another perspective emerges as to why believers *need* to participate in the local church. God has gifted each believer's brothers and sisters with unique abilities to aid in that believer's growth: "Each one should use whatever gift he has received to serve others, administering God's grace in its various forms" (1 Pet. 4:10);

"Now to each one the manifestation of the Spirit is given for the common good" (1 Cor. 12:7).

If each member of the Body of Christ is to thrive, there will have to be the presence of such things as teaching, pastoring, administration, service, encouragement, and hospitality. Each member of a church does not possess each of these gifts, but other members of the church do. To cut yourself off from fellow church members is to be cut off from what the Bible calls "God's grace in its various forms."

But it is not only the gifts of fellow Christians that bless the believer; the simple *bodily presence* of brothers and sisters is a blessing as well. Have you ever wondered why both Paul and Peter speak in their letters about the believers greeting one another "with a holy kiss"? Typically, these passages elicit a wink-wink, nudge-nudge response from younger listeners; but what significance do they hold for us? They remind us that the tangible presence of a church family, highlighted in *our* cultural setting by handshakes and hugs, does something in the core of our being that we profoundly need. Believers who have gone without such physical togetherness with other believers (POWs, for example) attest to the profound sense of loss they experienced from such deprivation.

This truth was powerfully demonstrated in the experience of a thriving Presbyterian church in the Midwest. After experiencing ongoing growth in membership, the church moved from one morning worship service to two services, then eventually to three. Before long, even these three services were insufficient to accommodate the numbers who were attending on Sunday mornings. It seemed inevitable that the sanctuary would have to be expanded, and the church leaders decided to begin the process of doing just that.

Since the expansion of the sanctuary made worship there impossible for a time, the church's multi-purpose building was temporarily used as the site for morning worship. This was not only a labor-intensive decision, since church members assisted in the setting up of hundreds of folding chairs, but one that placed the congregation in rather close quarters with each other. How did this affect participation on Sunday mornings? One might guess that the inconvenience and crowded conditions would negatively affect attendance, but, interestingly, the numbers of worshipers during this time actually *increased*.

Eventually, the sanctuary expansion was completed, and morning worship was resumed in its former location. As worshipers returned to their more familiar setting, they found a beautifully redone sanctuary that afforded considerably more room, as well as other improvements. What is surprising, though, is that upon this return, *the numbers of worshipers decreased*. The pews required no setting up on the part of the members, and the additional pews afforded more room for everyone, but with these improvements came a certain sense of loss. Apparently, being in close quarters had been a blessing.

The local church as God's community

Ultimately, God made us in His image, and God is in fellowship with Himself—as the Father, the Son, and the Holy Spirit. God enjoys fellowship in a never-ending, Trinitarian relationship. We were created to be like God. This takes us to the essence of why we should "belong" to a local church: The truth is that we were created to be in community with each other just as God is in community with Himself.

Some years ago a small-group Bible study for students was discussing ultimate issues in life. Quoting from the *Westminster Shorter Catechism*, "What is the chief end of man?" the group was asked why they thought God had created mankind. By far, the most popular response was, "Because He was lonely. God created man because He wanted someone to love and care for."

Was God somehow deficient in His essence so that He had to supplement His own existence with creatures to love? Theologians are quick to remind us that God lacks nothing in Himself. God is not needy. Even God owes His own existence to nothing beyond Himself. Theologians refer to this as God's *aseity,* or self-existence. An African-American minister once put it this way, "God is God . . . all by Himself!"

God did not create man because He was lonely, because He was, in fact, *not* lonely. God's very self-definition teaches that He existed from all eternity in utterly fulfilled fellowship. God was, and is, *connected* with the members of the Trinity. The relationship of Father, Son, and Holy Spirit is *the* archetypal relationship. Jonathan Edwards put it this way:

> And this I suppose to be the blessed Trinity that
> we read of in the Holy Scriptures. The Father is the
> deity subsisting in the prime, unoriginated and
> most absolute manner, or the deity in its direct exis-

tence. The Son is the deity generated by God's understanding, or having an idea of Himself and subsisting in that idea. The Holy Ghost is the deity subsisting in act, or the divine essence flowing out [of] and breathed forth in God's infinite love to delight in Himself. And I believe the whole Divine essence does truly and distinctly subsist both in the Divine idea and Divine love.[10]

Richard of St. Victor, a twelfth-century Scot living in France, wrote wonderfully about why God is a Trinity. Richard was particularly moved by passages that spoke of the love of God. The idea that "God is love" captivated him. Drawing from passages such as 1 Corinthians 13 and John 3:16, Richard noticed that biblical love is never self-centered; rather, it is always self-giving. Love is an overflowing and outgoing reality that always seeks to benefit that which is outside of itself. True love desires to fellowship with others and to care for others.

Therefore, since God is love, to think of Him in isolation is a contradiction. God has always existed in an internal fellowship of persons. Richard drew heavily from the passage in Ephesians 3 that says, "Father, from whom the whole family in heaven and earth is named." Fatherhood is rooted in God's essential being, such that He has never been without a Son.

The bond that exists between a father and son, then, is a pale reflection, an object lesson, of the fellowship of the Trinity. God created the institutions of marriage and family for the purpose of reflecting the reality of His own self-definition. Community and fellowship, relationships in general, have always existed. We are *formatted* for relationship.

The Church at-large, and the local church, are the natural manifestations of God's people in the process of being godly—in loving fellowship.

Painting with the broadest of strokes, Reformed theology says that the most faithful representation of the history of the Bible sees the Church's origin in the mind of God before the foundations of the Earth. God, in love, was making people in His image—fundamentally, people were to be in fellowship.

The purpose of all of human history is the development and glorification of this ultimate fellowship of God's called-out people, the Church. The people of God have taken varied apparent forms throughout redemptive history. Therefore, the nation of Israel *is* the Church in its infancy. When Jesus attended synagogue, in a very real sense He attended church just as you and I are to do.

John Calvin said that the Old Testament is a flickering candle compared to the burning bright beacon of the New. Pastor and author Steve Schissel once said, "The church wasn't born at Pentecost: it was bar mitzvah'd."

Paul says that the authority given by God to the Lord Jesus Christ was to fulfill his purposes in history "for the church." Ephesians 1:19b–23 sums up his conviction:

> That power is like the working of his mighty
> strength, which he exerted in Christ when he raised

him from the dead and seated him at his right hand in the heavenly realms, far above all rule and authority, power and dominion, and every title that can be given, not only in the present age but also in the one to come. And God placed all things under his feet and appointed him to be head over everything for the church, which is his body, the fullness of him who fills everything in every way.

This thought boggles the mind. Everything that God does in the world is for the Church-at-large and is to be enjoyed through fellowship in a local church. All talent, all insight, all beauty, all wisdom, and all discovery, whether from Christians or non-Christians, exist for the delight of the Church. All of the hidden potentialities that God has implanted in creation are gifts given from the Father to His children to relish and enjoy.

So the question really becomes: Why in the world wouldn't a person want to be a member of a local church?

But this may all seem a bit too tidy. The biblical evidence for why we need to be part of a local church is straightforward. We must admit, however, that the thing that drives people away from the local church is epidemic internal problems. Local churches, and the Church worldwide, are made up of sinners, and while fellowship is often sweet and imitates the fellowship of the Triune God, it is also incomplete. What if you join a church, and it seems to be a complete mess?

Visible Messiness

An interesting Bible study is to examine New Testament letters that were written to local churches and to compare the invisible Church language of a letter with the visible church descriptions within that same letter (what we might call the "Church/church dynamic").

Why is it worthwhile to do this? Because in doing so, we begin to see that the very same group of people that could be described in such *encouraging* ways could also be described as a group riddled with *discouraging* problems. As a brief example, consider Paul's letters to the local churches in Philippi, Galatia, and Corinth.

Seeing the Church/church dynamic within these letters will help us to see that God is always at work locally and globally. When local church members are interacting, they are part of a universal orchestra that God is conducting. Despite the dissonance we contribute, God smoothes out the totality into heavenly music. In fact, that is exactly what He is doing.

Groucho Marx once quipped: "I don't want to belong to any club that would have me as a member." The astounding thing is that God has invited you and me to be a part of His glorious Church, even though God knows we will come in and make a mess of things. Look now at three early local church examples and see how God's church members, though sinful, are used to fulfill God's plan.

Philippi

Paul's letter to the Philippians is addressed to "all the saints in

Christ Jesus at Philippi, together with the overseers and deacons" (1:1). Clearly, then, his intended audience is a body of true believers in Jesus Christ. He underscores this fact by referring to his readers as "brothers" at least six times and as "saints" twice. Apparently he has no exceptions in mind, since he states that *"all of you* share in God's grace with me" (1:7).[11]

Furthermore, he describes this group of Philippian believers in terms that can only be applied to the Church. Paul writes of their "partnership in the gospel from the first day until now" (1:5); he notes that "he who began a good work in you [plural] will carry it on to completion until the day of Christ Jesus" (1:6; cf. 2:13); he confidently asserts that they "have always obeyed—not only in my presence, but now much more in my absence" (2:12); and he mutually delights that "our citizenship is in heaven" and that "we eagerly await a Savior from there, the Lord Jesus Christ, who . . . will transform our lowly bodies so that they will be like his glorious body" (3:20–21).

It should be no surprise, then, that in the *very next* verse he describes this group in Philippi as "my brothers, you whom I love and long for, my joy and crown" (4:1).

What may be surprising, though, is what he says in the very next verse (and keep in mind that this would have been read *out loud* to this group of believers). Paul writes, "I plead with Euodia and I plead with Syntyche to agree with each other in the Lord."

What? Surely a group of people who are "saints" and whose "citizenship is in heaven" would not have two women in its midst who were unable to get along with each other! Surely the news of this breach of relationship would not travel all the way from Philippi to the site of Paul's imprisonment!

Apparently, though, they did, and it did. This group of beloved believers—saved by Christ and loved by Paul—actually had problems. Today, they are part of God's divine story used to instruct us toward godliness. God's Church fulfills God's plans.

Galatia

This letter is actually addressed to a group of local churches: "To the churches in Galatia" (1:2). Paul's tone throughout is one of confidence that those who will receive it are true believers. He states: "You are *all* sons of God through faith in Christ Jesus, for *all* of you who were baptized into Christ have clothed yourselves with Christ" (3:26-27; cf. 4:6-7).[12]

Later, he writes: "You, brothers, like Isaac, are children of promise" (4:28). Paul equates these Gentile believers with the favored line of Abraham! Elsewhere, he states that these believers have received the Holy Spirit (3:2, 5) and that they have been set free by Christ (5:1).

However, anyone who has read Galatians knows that it does not exactly read like a greeting card. On the contrary, it contains some of Paul's harshest language.

Paul even describes the recipients of his letter as "foolish" and as having been "bewitched" (3:1), primarily because they were willing to entertain notions of embracing "a different gospel—which is really no gospel at all" (1:6–7). He goes on to say to his readers that those "who are trying to be justified by law have been alienated from Christ; you have fallen away from grace" (5:4).

Later, he describes not only doctrinal error, but moral error as well. In 5:15 he warns: "If you keep on biting and devouring each other, watch out or you will be destroyed by each other." If Paul had to warn them against a *continued* pattern of infighting, it must have been going on at the time of his letter. How could local church members fight during Paul's life? They did—and they still do.

Toward the close of the letter, Paul also gives these directions: "Brothers, if someone is caught in a sin, you who are spiritual should restore him gently. But watch yourself, or you also may be tempted" (6:1). Paul not only wanted them to know what to do when church members strayed, but he also wanted them to beware the possibility of falling into the identical sin they were seeking to address.

So again, we see this tension (if we may call it that) within the churches of Galatia. Paul could simultaneously describe the recipients of this letter as both "sons of God through faith in Christ Jesus" *and* as "foolish." He could assure them that they were "like Isaac . . . children of promise" *and* then rebuke some of them for "trying to be justified by law." The churches of Galatia were groups of real believers in real fellowship—with real problems.

Corinth

For the supreme example of the Church/church dynamic in Paul's letters, however, pride of place must go to the church in Corinth. For the sake of brevity, we will confine ourselves to Paul's *first* letter to this local church.

Paul addresses this long letter to "the church of God in Corinth, to those sanctified in Christ Jesus and called to be holy" (1:2). He goes on to offer this word of thanksgiving about them:

> I always thank my God for you because of his grace given you in Christ Jesus. For in him you have been enriched in every way—in all your speaking and in all your knowledge—because our testimony about Christ was confirmed in you. Therefore you do not lack any spiritual gift as you eagerly wait for our Lord Jesus Christ to be revealed. He will keep you strong to the end, so that you will be blameless on the day of our Lord Jesus Christ (1:4–8).

Later, he expresses to the Corinthians his assurance that "you were washed, you were sanctified, you were justified in the name of the Lord Jesus Christ and by the Spirit of our God" (6:11). Elsewhere, he describes them as "God's temple," indwelt by the Holy Spirit (3:16; cf. 6:19), and as "the body of Christ," going on to say that *"each one of you is a part of it"* (12:27).[13]

It should also be noted that Paul's language in this letter reveals the utmost affection. He not only refers to the Corinthians as his "brothers" throughout but also refers to them as "my dear children" (4:14), "my dear friends" (10:14), and "my dear brothers" (15:58). He closes the letter with these words: "My love to all of you in Christ Jesus" (16:24).

But you already know where this is going! Space hardly allows for an adequate treatment of all the problems in the Corinthian church that Paul addresses. Among them are divisive "quarrels" (1:11–12; cf. 11:17–18), being "worldly" (3:1–3), arrogance (4:18), lawsuits between believers (6:6-8), wounding one another's conscience (8:9–12), misuse of the Lord's Supper—even to the point of drunkenness (11:20–21), and a disbelief (by some) in the resurrection of the dead (15:12).

Undoubtedly, the most heinous example of all is an incestuous relationship that had developed between a man and "his father's wife" (5:1ff). This is so disturbing that one might think that Paul is describing a matter in the community, not the church itself.

However, he goes on to clarify that very point: "What business is it of mine to judge those outside the church? Are you not to judge those *inside?* God will judge those outside. 'Expel the wicked man *from among you'*" (5:12-13).[14] The cruel reality is that this problem, and the others as well, were the messy problems of the *Christian Church* of Corinth.

Christ cleanses the Church

The examples above are not an exercise in redundancy. The point must be underscored. *The Church, the body of Christ, is presently manifested in visible groups of believers who have very real problems and who will disappoint some of our expectations.* Our temptation is to read the biblical descriptions of the invisible Church, look around at the state of affairs in the local church, and conclude that these must be two unrelated groups of people. This is an unbiblical conclusion.

God, in His kindness, has not merely left us with beautiful descriptions of the Church in the Scriptures, but also with painfully honest descriptions of what local bodies of believers look like. Negligence of either biblical depiction will lead to unhealthy views of the bride of Christ.

But this is clear: If you want to be a part of Christ's wonderful cleansing work, the local church is the place to be. This is where His heart is, and this is where He pledges to love us in our messiness.

◆ ◆ ◆

In his classic work *The Screwtape Letters,* C. S. Lewis presents a series of letters written by an older, seasoned devil, Screwtape, to his younger, inexperienced nephew, Wormwood. Each letter deals with how Wormwood handles his "patient" (the individual he is seeking to ruin spiritually).

In his second letter, Screwtape offers this advice to his nephew:

> One of our great allies at present is the Church itself. Do not misunderstand me. I do not mean the Church as we see her spread out through all time and space and rooted in eternity, terrible as an army with banners. That, I confess, is a spectacle that makes our boldest tempters uneasy. But fortunately

it is quite invisible to these humans. All your patient sees is the half-finished, sham Gothic erection on the new building estate . . . When he gets to his pew and looks round him he sees just that selection of his neighbours whom he has hitherto avoided. You want to lean pretty heavily on those neighbours. Make his mind flit to and fro between an expression like "the body of Christ" and the actual faces in the next pew . . . Provided that any of those neighbours sing out of tune, or have boots that squeak, or double chins, or odd clothes, the patient will quite easily believe that their religion must therefore be somehow ridiculous. At his present stage, you see, he has an idea of "Christians" in his mind which he supposes to be spiritual but which, in fact, is largely pictorial. His mind is full of togas and sandals and armour and bare legs and the mere fact that the other people in church wear modern clothes is a real—though of course an unconscious—difficulty to him. Never let it come to the surface; never let him ask what he expected them to look like.[15]

This is an unsettling passage.

Something about these words rings true within us. We know what it is to hear noble things about the Church-at-large ("terrible as an army with banners"), and we know what it is to want such noble themes to be true. Sadly, though, we also know the processes within our own hearts as we have looked around at other professing believers ("the actual faces in the next pew") and thought, "Whoever makes up the Church, they can't be like this."

But wait a minute. Who are we to be put off by messiness in the local church? Have we forgotten that when we participate in a body of believers, *we bring our own messiness into the mix?* As the saying goes, "Of course the Church will always have hypocrites in it—we joined!"

Perhaps that is the fundamental problem. If we are ruthlessly honest about how the Scriptures depict *our own* hearts, we must admit that any group that would "have" us must be one that is, and will be, marked by observable, messy problems. Often, though, that is an admission that we are unwilling to make.

Here, however, is the good news: One of the most beautiful descriptions of the Church to be found in all of Scripture proclaims the reality of the Church's "stains" and "blemishes" and the glorious remedy as well. "Christ loved the church and gave himself up for her to make her holy, cleansing her by the washing with water through the word, and to present her to himself as a radiant church, without stain or wrinkle or any other blemish, but holy and blameless" (Eph. 5:25–27).

Christ did not love the Church because He came to her and found her beautiful. He loved her despite her obvious foulness and, in His love, has achieved her beautification. He did not do so for an abstract, imaginary bride. He did so for real, earthy believers—the same people that are to be found, and *should* be found, in the local church.

4

The Business of the Church

"The greatest issue facing the church of the twentieth century concerns the church's definition of its own nature and mission."[1]

~ O. Palmer Robertson

"So the Twelve gathered all the disciples together and said, 'It would not be right for us to neglect the ministry of the word of God in order to wait on tables. Brothers, choose seven men from among you who are known to be full of the Spirit and wisdom. We will turn this responsibility over to them and will give our attention to prayer and the ministry of the word.'"

~ The Book of Acts

"I have an idea," said a friend, his impish smile indicating there was a point to his antics.

"I want to open a used car lot at the church," he continued.

Huh?

"Yeah, think of it. It'll be great. We have all that parking lot space left mostly vacant throughout the week. We'll simply move the cars off the lot on Sundays for church and sell cars the rest of the week. It'll give Christians a place where they can buy their cars and give an opportunity for them to witness to lost people who come to the lot looking."

I decided to play along with the game just to see where he was headed. *Well, who will run the used car lot?*

"I will, and you can help me if you want. But we'll need to have the elders of our church oversee it."

All of a sudden, it was clear where this friend was going. Why in the world would the church take on a project like a used car lot? Why would the elders waste their time overseeing something that is so clearly removed from their biblical job description? This friend was getting at a core church issue: just what is okay and is not okay for the church to do? A basketball gym? A school? A shopping mall? (All of these are now being run by American churches.) What would keep a church from opening a pawnshop, or a legal office, or a doctor's office, or an accountant's office?

"Great question," this wise friend said, a grin spilling over his face. "Kinda makes you wonder about a lot of things the Church does, doesn't it?"

There is a constant refrain coming from more socially aware believers that usually goes like this: "Well, if the Church was doing its job, then we wouldn't need such and such an organization to do it for us."

Of course, what the critic often fails to recognize is that if the Church consists of all those who proclaim Jesus as Savior and Lord, then to level this charge is to point the finger at oneself, because the Church is made up of you.

But this is not what they mean. Such critics mean that the problem is not with the individuals in the Church, but that the Church-at-large *as an institution* and the local church are not doing their job.

This criticism raises many questions and begs clarification.

- What is the Church's job?
- How does she know when she is or is not "doing her job"?
- By what standard will her job performance be evaluated?

The Church struggles today with the same issue that faces many CEOs of major corporations—namely, that without a clear statement of the organization's mission, the company flounders in its productivity.

For most American evangelicals, the Church's job description consists of an almost endless list of tasks that are as varied as the people who insist upon them. For many the Church exists primarily as a necessary social outlet. Others insist that the Church perform the function of social-welfare provider. Still others rely upon the Church to be the preserver of their personal tradition or a haven for their children in a culture of crisis.

However, Reformation history has stressed that the marks of the Church consist of the faithful preaching of the Word, the right administration of the Sacraments, and the consistent exercise of Godly discipline, which we will develop more fully in the second half of this chapter.

Almost no one would object to these. No one is busy mounting great theological protests against these activities in the Church (if they are taking place at all!). However, the questions arise about the "other things." What about "other things" that can certainly be considered appropriate Christian responsibilities but are outside the purview of the Word, Sacraments, and Discipline?

"Kingdom" and "Church": *There is a difference*

At this point, it is necessary to introduce a distinction.

The key to grasping an understanding of the business of the Church rests upon the Scriptures' distinction between the Church and the Kingdom of God. Throughout the New Testament, the terms refer to different ideas. Jesus' first sermons would make no sense if the ideas of the Kingdom of God and the Church were equated, "Repent, for the Church is at hand." Likewise, the first missionaries preached the Kingdom of God, not the Church (Acts 8:12; 19:8; 20: 25; 28:23; 31). Obviously, these early Christians saw a difference between the two concepts.

But to what do these terms refer if they are indeed distinct?

The Church

The Church, as we have said, is God's *ekklesia* (literally in Greek, His "called out ones"). The term refers to the gathering of those redeemed by the blood of Jesus. The Church is the elect from before the foundations of the earth; the called of God, redeemed by the Son, and indwelt of the Holy Spirit. However, these redeemed individuals take on certain characteristics as they gather. *They become an institution, a society, an establishment, a body.* There is organization to them *when they gather together.* This association is what we call the Church.

The Kingdom

However, when Christians live their lives in the world, that life is lived in the Kingdom (*basilea*) of God. Of course, the Kingdom of God is related to the Church. Membership in the Church, by definition, includes membership and participation in the Kingdom. However, the Kingdom of God encompasses a broader realm.

When the phrase "Kingdom of God" appears in the New Testament, it refers to the place where God's sovereign rule in principle *comes to concrete expression:* God's revealed and living kingship over all of life. The Kingdom of God certainly includes what is done in the Church, but the Kingdom of God extends to what is done in one's family, in one's vocation, and even in one's heart. The believer can no more excuse himself from Kingdom life than he can be a Christian and not united to Christ.

Therefore, whenever the Spirit of God overtakes a heart and holiness of life and rightness of character are manifest, the Kingdom of God has come.

Whenever Christians band together to stop the opening of an adult bookstore in their neighborhood, the Kingdom of God has come.

Whenever a Christian businessman decides that he will no longer continue to run his business through worldly practices and deceitful scheming, the Kingdom of God has come.

Jesus said to the Pharisees in Matthew 12:28, "But if I cast out demons by the Spirit of God, then the kingdom of God has come upon you." At any point in which God's actual rule comes to expression over evil and sin, there is the Kingdom of God. New Testament theologian G. E. Ladd concludes this about the relationship between the Kingdom of God and the Church:

> The Kingdom creates the church, works through the church, and is proclaimed in the world by the church. There can be no Kingdom without a church—those who have acknowledged God's rule—and there can be no church without God's Kingdom; but *they remain two distinguishable concepts: the rule of God and the fellowship of men.*[2]

The Church amidst the Kingdom

Why is this relevant to our discussion on the business of the Church? Because the first believers understood that if the Church was to maintain the integrity of her mission in the world and not forget her primary calling, she must withdraw from activities not specific to her sphere and commit herself to the jobs that God had given only her to do.

In Acts 6, the disciples make some vital decisions regarding the division of labor in the early church.

> So the Twelve gathered all the disciples together and said, "It would not be right for us to neglect the ministry of the word of God in order to wait on

tables. Brothers, choose seven men from among you who are known to be full of the Spirit and wisdom. We will turn this responsibility over to them and will give our attention to prayer and the ministry of the word" (v. 2-4).

Clearly the disciples saw a vital difference between "ministry of the word of God" on the one hand and "waiting on tables" on the other. The first activity was spiritual in nature. The Word had to be preached in order for lives to be changed and hearts to be converted. So fundamental was this activity to the life of the church that nothing was to be allowed to distract them from its practice.

In other words, the disciples self-consciously withdrew from certain activities so that they could concentrate on responsibilities directly related to their sphere. So committed were the disciples to these primary activities that they instituted an entire office dedicated to the temporal, or physical, needs of the church. The office is known as the diaconate. The Apostles had jobs; the deacons had jobs. And in order to be effective in ministry, there could not be a confusion of the two.

The principle also applies to the Kingdom and the Church. One of the most difficult challenges that the Church at the dawn of the 21st century will have to face is the twin temptation to venture into spheres of activity that are beyond her pale, on the one hand, while, on the other hand, to abandon her charter as the keeper of the marks of the Church.

Responsibilities in the Kingdom of God need to remain in the hands of Christians who inhabit those spheres, while the responsibilities within the Church need to remain at the feet of those gifted by God and ordained by the body to do so. Kingdom and Church must mind their respective business.

God has given the authority to execute the ministry of the Word, Sacraments and Discipline *to the Church alone.* There is no other organization mentioned in Scripture with the authority to act as caretaker of these marks. And yet Christians have somehow assumed that all worthwhile Christian service that is done in the world must be funneled through the local assembly of believers. Dutch theologian Louis Berkof sums it up this way:

> It is also a mistake to maintain, as some Reformed Christians do, in virtue of an erroneous conception of the Church as an organism, that Christian school societies, voluntary organizations of younger or older people for the study of Christian principles and their application in life, Christian labor unions, and Christian political organizations, are *manifestations of the Church as an organism,* for this again brings them under the domain of the visible Church and under the direct control of its officers. Naturally, this does not mean that the Church has no responsibility with respect to such organizations. It does mean, however, that they are manifestations of the Kingdom of God, in

which groups of Christians seek to apply the principles of the Kingdom to every domain of life.[3]

For example, following Berkof, we could just as easily ask a question about the Church in the medical field. Should it be the responsibility of the courts of the Church to start and administer hospitals?
Where in Paul's instruction to Timothy and Titus regarding the
responsibilities of elders is hospital administration? (1 Timothy 3; cf.
Titus 1) Suddenly, my friend's question has become quite relevant,
"Kinda makes you wonder about a lot of things the Church does,
doesn't it?"

Make no mistake; it *is* the responsibility of *Christians* to start and
administrate hospitals. However, it is decidedly *not* the responsibility
of pastors and elders *in their corporate capacity* to take responsibility for
these kinds of works. Stated another way, hospital administration is
Kingdom work, a sphere in which every Christian lives and is
required to serve.

On the other hand, is it ever right for the Church to turn over
her responsibilities to other organizations when the task has been
laid at her feet? John Murray, Scottish theologian of Westminster
Seminary, comments on evangelistic societies that have no oversight from the Church.

> Far be it from any of us to deny the fruits that
> have accrued from these evangelistic activities in
> the conversion of souls and the extension of the
> kingdom of God. But sincerity and zeal are not the

criteria of propriety, nor is the conversion of souls the guarantee that the methods used have divine sanction . . . It is true that the organized church has oftentimes been apathetic and failed to carry out the demands of commission. But *the remedy is not to abandon the church* as the agent and instrument of mission, but to institute and pursue measures whereby all rightful and urgent zeal for evangelism can receive its outlet through the medium and in the solidarity of the church as the body of Christ.[4]

The careful distinctions being made here may obscure the almost innumerable count of benefits arising from this way of thinking about the business of the Church. The distinction is deeply practical.

First, this idea should serve as the impetus for pastors to be pastors again. They can focus their efforts, just as the Apostles did, on ministry of the Word, prayer, and spiritual oversight. In so doing, there might just be a drop in the alarming rate of burnout among many clergymen.

Second, church members just might be roused out of their slumber when it comes to activity within the Kingdom. Jesus does not allow for Christians to be such only behind the four walls of the building that they refer to as "church." They too easily associate "ministry" with what happens in a *place,* not what happens in every area of life. Perhaps this is the only way to explain the almost maddening urge most churches have to undertake building projects. "If ministry is going to happen, then we need more space . . . more buildings." Granted, there is nothing wrong with buildings per se, but it is the spirit that seems inevitably to accompany these building projects that ought to give the people of God pause.

Jesus Christ is Lord over every area of life for the Christian; therefore, there is no area of life that escapes His direction. For a man to shake his head and say, *"Tsk, tsk,* someone ought to do something about those poor homeless men downtown," is to admit that he has seen a need and not taken the responsibility to meet it. Instead, he attends the next Wednesday-night prayer meeting and suggests that a committee of the church be formed in order to "look into" the "possibility" of "considering" something being done about the poor in his neighborhood!

"Do it yourself!" ought to be the Church's cry. "Band together with the believers with whom you sit side by side, Sunday after Sunday, and do something about bringing justice to the world."

The diaconate formed in Acts 6 was given for the purpose of ministry to the poor *within her sphere,* that is, within the Church. They were associated for the purpose of meeting the physical needs of those who were *believers.*[5] "Well, that's just the church. Who is going to minister to the needs of the poor in the world?" you ask.[6]

"Every single Christian!" is Jesus' answer.

As a matter of fact, Matthew 25:31ff. seems to suggest that the very criterion that Jesus will use to separate the "sheep" from the "goats" at the final judgment will be based upon their personal and associated involvement with the poor, the naked, the incarcerated, and the hungry.

> Then he will say to those on his left, 'Depart
> from me, you who are cursed, into the eternal fire
> prepared for the devil and his angels. For I was hun-
> gry and you gave me nothing to eat, I was thirsty
> and you gave me nothing to drink, I was a stranger
> and you did not invite me in, I needed clothes and
> you did not clothe me, I was sick and in prison and
> you did not look after me.' They also will answer,
> 'Lord, when did we see you hungry or thirsty or a
> stranger or needing clothes or sick or in prison, and
> did not help you?' He will reply, 'I tell you the
> truth, whatever you did not do for one of the least
> of these, you did not do for me.'

The responsibility to relieve suffering around them rests squarely in the lap of all who name the name of Christ. It is a *sine qua non* of Christianity. But it is decidedly not solely the responsibility of pastors and elders, *as pastors and elders*. Remember, even pastors and elders are members of the Kingdom, and responsibilities for the Kingdom in their spheres of influence are no less real than in their parishioners. How easy and dangerous it is for a minister to assume that, because his vocation is the Church, he has fulfilled his responsibility in the Kingdom.

This may sound unnecessarily confusing to some. Is a pastor

always to be asking which hat he is wearing at any given moment in his work? The answer, of course, is "no." For example, there is rarely a confusion of roles when we are dealing with the sphere of the family. When a man takes his son to work with him, he instinctively knows what actions are appropriate as "father" and what actions are appropriate as "businessman." He knows them because he is so familiar with the nature of these two spheres. Our point here is that the instincts of Christendom regarding the Church's sphere are not so refined, and need to be informed by the direction of the Apostles in Acts 6.

The Marks of the Church

There are few more dramatic (and pivotal) scenes in the synoptic Gospels than Jesus' interchange with His disciples as they answer His question, "Who do men say that I am?" After getting the word on the street, he then asks, "But who do you say that I am?" Peter answers, "You are the Christ, the Son of the living God" (Matt. 16). Peter confesses that Jesus is the Messiah, or the "Anointed One."

There is not a whole lot of "anointing" that goes on in our day, but in the Old Testament, the practice was common. Anointing was used to set apart a person for an office, a job or a role. A quick look through the Old Testament will show that there were three offices to which someone could be "anointed."

First, prophets were anointed. A prophet was someone who, very simply, came with a message from God to the people (cf. Deut. 18:18, 1 Kings 19:16). Isaiah says of himself (a passage that Jesus would later claim as his own), "The Spirit of the Sovereign Lord is on me, because the Lord has *anointed* me to preach good news to the poor. He has sent me to bind up the brokenhearted, to proclaim freedom for the captives and release from darkness for the prisoner" (16:1). [Emphasis added]

Second, priests were anointed. If the prophet was God's representative to the people, then the priest was man's representative to God. He could speak and act on behalf of the people. In Exodus 40:13, God commands Moses to "dress Aaron in the sacred garments, *anoint* him and consecrate him so he may serve Me as priest."

Third, kings were anointed. A king possessed headship, authority, and judgment. He was to rule over his subjects fairly with justice and equity. When Samuel saw the soon-to-be-king David, the Lord commanded him, "Rise and *anoint* him; he is the one" (1 Sam. 16:12).

Therefore, as Peter spoke his famous line to Jesus, he was saying much more than "you are an important person." Peter was saying that in this man, Jesus, all of the Old Testament offices of prophet, priest, and king are met and fulfilled! The Old Testament clearly predicted that every one of these offices would be filled by an archetype, or ultimate figure (Prophet, cf. Deut. 18:15; Priest, cf. Zech. 6:13; King, cf. Psalm 45:6,7). Shivers must have run up and down the spine of the other disciples as they weighed the magnitude of Peter's statement.

It is quite interesting, though, that Jesus chooses this moment to teach about His Church. It is after this confession that Jesus is the long awaited Anointed One that Jesus says He will build His Church (Matt. 16:18). His people will have His anointing as her very foundation of being. Jesus will be her one and only head, and He will rule as the great Prophet, Priest, and King of His people.

Race forward in time to the year 1560, at the dawn of the Reformation in Scotland. Six "Johns" were busy at work producing what would become known as the *First Book of Discipline*. John Knox, John Willock, John Winram, John Spottiswoods, John Douglas, and John Row were wrestling with the question of the marks of a truly biblical church. What is the "true Church?" How could it be distinguished from the "false Church?" They had already committed themselves to two gigantic principles as they set their hands to the task: "That neither ye admit anything which God's plain Word shall not approve, and neither yet that ye shall reject such ordinances as equity, justice, and God's Word do specify."

Their work produced the following conclusions: The true Church is to be identified by the true preaching of the Word of God; the right administration of the sacraments; and church discipline "uprightly administered as God in His Word prescribes, whereby vice is repressed and virtue nourished."

These three marks set the standard for the rest of the Reformation as the Reformers contemplated the identity of the Church.

So why were these marks identified and not others? Are there not other aspects of the Church that belong in this list? What about worship, or works of service?

It is vital to remember that Christ exercises His headship over His Church through his three anointed offices.

- As prophet, He guards God's words to man.

- As priest he protects man's representation before God.
- As King, he watches over and protects His people.

Therefore, the three marks of the Church are the Word (Prophet), the Sacraments (Priest), and Discipline (King).

In order for Christ to exercise complete headship over His people, He must do so through His offices. G. I. Williamson, in his commentary on the *Westminster Shorter Catechism* says, "This is why the marks of the true Church must be the faithful preaching of the word of God, the true administration of the sacraments, and the faithful exercise of Church discipline. In these things we see the glorious fulfillment of Christ's ministry as prophet, priest, and king."[7]

Therefore, a consideration of these marks of the Church is vital to our understanding of the business of the Church.

Mark No. 1: *True biblical preaching*

The Church is first distinguished by the *true preaching of the Word of God*. Few places in Holy Scripture more clearly set forth the absolute necessity of the proclamation of the Word than Luke 16:19–31, the parable of the Rich Man and Lazarus. The story is familiar. The Rich Man, because he looks down on the poor and refuses to meet the needs of Lazarus who sits at his very gates, lands himself in the torments of hell.

Most commentators center their exposition of this passage on our Lord's description of perdition and judgment; however, the conclusion of the story packs the real punch. After a brief discussion with

Father Abraham concerning the inescapability of his situation, the Rich Man appears to grow a heart, albeit too late. "I beg you, father, send Lazarus to my father's house, for I have five brothers. Let him warn them, so that they will not also come to this place of torment." Father Abraham's response appears abrupt, "They have Moses and the Prophets; let them listen to them."

The phrase "Moses and the Prophets," of course, refers to the Hebrew Old Testament, the "Scriptures" to that day and age. The Rich Man then decides to correct father Abraham's misunderstanding, "No, father Abraham, but if someone from the dead goes to them, they will repent."

The Rich Man's logic seems compelling. Imagine attending an open-casket funeral where halfway through the service the cadaver sits up and starts to speak. At the least, the dead man speaking would command an attentive audience. But Father Abraham is insistent: "If they do not listen to Moses and the Prophets, they will not be convinced even if someone rises from the dead."

There are enormous implications emerging from what Jesus says here.

First, Jesus is asserting that mankind's condition in sin is so severe that even his mind cannot be trusted. Direct exposure to the truth is no guarantee that man will do the right thing with that truth. The catchall solution, it seems, to every societal ill in our day is the ambiguous "education." If young people know the risks involved in premarital sex, then they will be less likely to engage in it, we are told. If children are made aware of the dangers of recreational drug use, then they are equipped to "just say no" when appropriate.

Second, however, Jesus seems to be saying that the facts do not always speak for themselves. It is not enough to draw men into righteous living by cleverly devised ministry plans and church-growth strategies, much less into the Kingdom of God. Only the Word of God possesses the power to do this. Paul speaks of the gospel in Romans 1:16 and says, "It is the power of God for the salvation of everyone who believes." Notice, Paul does not say that the gospel talks about power, or shows the way to get power, but is *itself* the power. The power is in the proclamation of the message.

God's powerful Word represents the vital aspect of the Church's existence. The Word of God is not only her charter; it is her life (cf. Deut. 32:47). John Armstrong, editor of *The Coming Evangelical Crisis*, says this about the Church's present attitude toward the Word of God:

> The written Scriptures are to be our guide for message and method. We go to the Scriptures to understand the gospel, but we also go to the Scriptures to understand how we evangelize, how we preach, how we help the souls of distressed people, and how we worship the living and true God acceptably. Today we go to many sources to address these and related issues . . .
>
> Today's evangelicalism treats experience as final authority. Have you been born again? Have you been led by God? Has God spoken to your heart? Did you feel good about the worship (praise, cele-

bration, or seeker) service? Does the music move you personally? Are your kids excited about the programs? Rarely do we examine matters of religious faith and practice by the Scripture-alone principle.[8]

A local church without this utter dependence upon and submission to God's Word is no church at all. In times past, battles fought over the Bible centered on its reliability and inerrancy. But the challenge facing this generation of the Church-at-large must certainly involve the *relevancy* and *sufficiency* of the Scriptures.

Current theological "hot topics" such as the role of the Holy Spirit in worship and supernatural gifts, the "literalness" of prophetic pronouncements, and the date and circumstances surrounding the return of the Lord Jesus are all woefully premature. Until the Church at the dawn of the 21st century has settled itself on *this* issue—the sufficiency of Scripture—and, correspondingly, the absolute necessity of biblical preaching, there is little hope that any theological consensus will result from the myriad of denominations active today.

Mark No. 2: *The sacraments.*

The second mark of the Church is a *right administration of the sacraments.* Regardless of where a believer falls in his convictions concerning the Lord's Supper and Christian baptism, there can be little doubt that our spiritual forebears placed a far higher importance upon these means of grace than the present generation.

Ronald Wallace, in his work *Calvin's Doctrine of the Word and*

Sacrament, quotes Calvin as saying that there is "nothing more use-ful" in the Church than the Lord's Supper:

> Indeed, Calvin is willing to transfer to the sacra-ments Paul's title for the Gospel, and to call them the power of God unto salvation to everyone that believeth. He refers particularly to three aspects of their usefulness. Firstly, they assist spiritual growth by uniting us more fully to Christ the more they are used by faith . . . Secondly, they confirm and increase the faith of believers, which, once engen-dered, is so continually beset by temptation to doubt and by manifold difficulties that it requires to be continually supported and continually purged from unbelief . . . Thirdly, the sacraments are a spur to practical Christian living.[9]

However, it would be wrong to suppose that a believer's responsi-bility toward the sacraments is purely pragmatic or to make a person happier and healthier. The Lord's Supper and Baptism exist as essen-tial elements in the life of the Church because Christ Himself has instituted that it should be so.

First Corinthians 11:23 contains Paul's justification for the admo-nition to keep the Lord's Supper, "For I received from the Lord what I also passed on to you . . ." The sacraments are not an ordinance of man, but an ordinance of Jesus himself. To neglect them involves the guilt of rebellion, for Jesus commanded, "Do this in remembrance of me" (Luke 22:19b). Peter's command to the first believers at Pentecost was unequivocal: "Repent and be baptized, every one of you" (Acts 2:38).

Right administration of baptism

The grace of baptism has been woefully neglected in the Church today. Baptism, according to the *Westminster Shorter Catechism,* "doth signify and seal our ingrafting into Christ, and partaking of the benefits of the covenant of grace, and our engagement to be the Lord's."[10] As a sign, baptism points to something vital in the believer's life. As a seal, it makes official in the eyes of God and the Church that what is being done is truly a means of grace. The Catechism mentions three benefits that are signed and sealed in our baptism.

First, baptism signs and seals our "ingrafting into Christ." There are few notions in the thinking of the apostle Paul that get more "press" than the idea of union with Christ. When the Holy Spirit regenerates a believer, he is brought "into the Beloved" or "in Christ" (cf. Eph. 1:3ff). We are joined to Him like stones in a building (Eph. 2:19–22). We are like members of a body connected to our Head, Jesus Christ (Eph. 4:15–16). Our union with Christ resembles the union between a man and a woman in marriage (Eph. 5:22–33). John Murray, in his book *Redemption: Accomplished and Applied,* says, "There is no communion among men that is comparable to fellowship with Christ—he communes with his people in conscious reciprocal love."[11]

Our baptism signifies and seals this vital union.

Second, baptism marks a soul as a member of the covenant of grace. In Luke 15, the father begs the elder brother to make use of all that has been provided for him. "'My son,' the father said, 'you are always with me, and everything I have is yours'" (v. 31). The father here pleads with his oldest to make use of what has been provided for him in the community of the covenant of grace. Access to the Word of God, the instruction of godly parents, and involvement with the body of Christ—all are gifts at the disposal of those who are brought into the covenant by baptism. This, by the way, is why the *Westminster Confession of Faith* speaks so strongly about the necessity of "fulfilling one's baptism." To whom much is given, much is required. To have access to the abundant means of grace in the covenant community and not make use of them is to invite a more severe judgment.

Third, baptism signs and signifies our "engagement to be the Lord's." The Catechism's language turns deeply affectionate here. To submit oneself to water baptism is to anticipate a wedding. Every baptism signifies the great Marriage Supper of the Lamb that will take place at the consummation of all things. In Revelation 19:9, the angel tells John to write, "Blessed are those who are invited to the wedding supper of the Lamb!" Witnessing a Christian baptism reminds the covenant community that at the end of our days a *party* of cosmic proportions will take place as Jesus takes His bride to be His own forever.

Right administration of the Lord's Supper

The catechism also contains instruction concerning the meaning of the Lord's Supper as well:

> The Lord's supper is a sacrament, wherein, by
> giving and receiving bread and wine, according to
> Christ's appointment, his death is showed forth;
> and the worthy receivers are, not after a corporal
> and carnal manner, but by faith, made partakers of
> his body and blood, with all his benefits, to their
> spiritual nourishment, and growth in grace.[12]

There is far too much careful theology in this definition to examine, but notice that this sacrament is a meal. The Lord Jesus has appointed us to eat in order to our "partaking of his body and blood." Believers who do so receive enormous benefits and "spiritual nourishment."

While I was an unmarried seminary student, my roommates and I would practice our best "pitiful, hungry seminary student look" on the way to Sunday worship. Because if Providence smiled upon us that morning, some kind, elderly lady would ask us to her home for "Sunday supper." My fondest memories from seminary are of those wonderful afternoons. I had no more in common with those sitting around the gracious table than the fact that we attended the same church. We would eat until we were stuffed. But, inevitably, on the way back to our apartments, my friends and I would spend the entire time in unabashed praise of the sweet elderly lady who had just fed us.

The spirit of the Lord's Supper is much the same. How often does the Church take pause to remember that, in the Supper, she dines with her Lord? To eat a meal at someone else's home is a true act of intimacy. You eat what they have provided. You enjoy their topics of conversation. You observe their mealtime traditions. It is to become a member of the family. The Lord's Supper consists in the Lord's people gathered together to delight in the "richest of fare," namely the grace of Jesus in the shedding of His blood.

A Church without the sacraments is not only woefully impoverished, but it also fails to achieve the status of "Church" at all.

Mark No. 3: *Church discipline*

Finally, the third mark of the Church is *church discipline*. Few words have gained such disfavor in the Church in recent days as the word "discipline." The word seems to conjure up images of monasteries and cat o' nine tails for most Christians. It is true: discipline may be—and, at times, has been—used as an excuse for authoritarian rule and loveless tyranny. However, in the New Testament, church discipline is a far richer concept.

The word "discipline" might be substituted with the word "oversight." Church discipline is simply the responsibility that leadership has to oversee the spiritual health and well being of those in their pastoral care. Formally speaking, Paul directs Titus to "appoint elders in every town" (1:5b). Therefore, the direct, institutional oversight of the Church rests in the hands of those to whom God has especially gifted and appointed to do so, namely, to elders. (This directive is more fully addressed in chapter 6 on the submission of the Church.)

Yet there is another sense in which church discipline ought to be present in our churches. In Galatians 6:1 Paul directs, "Brothers, if someone is caught in a sin, you who are spiritual should restore him gently. But watch yourself, or you also may be tempted. Carry each other's burdens, and in this way you will fulfill the law of Christ." In other words, church discipline is not merely a formal exercise of bringing someone before a body of elders, but it is also a responsibility of all believers to be about the business of mutual spiritual welfare.

Eugene Peterson, in his book *Working the Angles,* describes what he calls "spiritual direction":

> Spiritual direction takes place when two people agree to give their full attention to what God is doing in one (or both) of their lives and seek to respond in faith. ... Whether planned or unplanned, three convictions underpin these meetings: 1) God is always doing something: an active grace is shaping this life into a mature salvation; 2) responding to God is not sheer guesswork: the Christian community has acquired wisdom through the centuries that provides guidance; 3) each soul is unique: no wisdom can simply be applied without discerning the particulars of this life, this situation.[13]

"God is at work," Peterson says. We can assume that at all times. Believers are either moving towards or moving away from God's purposes in their lives.

"No believer is alone," Peterson says. Our fierce individualism has not muted the fact that we live with a "great cloud of witnesses" to whom has been given great wisdom about so many of life's issues.

"Focus on the individual," Peterson stresses. Avoid stereotyping people by assuming that your ministry-model "works every time." People are infinitely complex and the Kingdom of God will never thrive under a method–driven ministry. We must be able to respond to all of life's vicissitudes with eternal verities emerging from the Scriptures and the wisdom of the ages that lives in subjection to them.

But for our purposes, we must grasp the spirit of church discipline if we are ever to identify it in our churches. Jesus describes the formal use of church discipline in Matthew 18:15ff. "If your brother sins against you, go and show him his fault, just between the two of you. If he listens to you, you have won your brother over."

Notice that the goal of oversight is to "win over your brother." Jesus' language places a watchdog over our motives as we take it upon ourselves to approach our brother to "show him his fault." Church discipline is not an excuse to air grievances, but a grace that God gives to bring about unity in the body. The questions we must ask are: "Do I long to be in right fellowship with this believer? How glad will I be if they do indeed repent? Am I punishing this person? Am I exacting revenge?" Therefore, the spirit of church discipline has restoration as its goal and longs for the connectedness that comes from perpetually repentant people.

Consequently, and second, church discipline exists with an

accompanying (and healthy) mistrust of self. It is our condition in sin that has created our need for oversight. Sin's greatest mischief in the life of a believer is to mask its own existence, to make us think that it is not there. The soul that has been most hardened by sin is the soul that thinks it is immune or untouched by its pollution. Therefore, the Gospel teaches us not to give ourselves the benefit of the doubt. We cannot be trusted on our own. If left to our own devices, our destruction would be certain.

Therefore, the inertia in the Church will always tend toward disintegration. The mark of the Church of discipline is therefore not only a theological necessity but a practical necessity as well. We need the Church, yes; but we need the Church *together*, involved in each other's lives, engaging in each other's business. Only this humility of community can set in motion the perpetual equipping of the saints and conversion of the lost for which the church exists. Without church discipline, there is no Church.

◆ ◆ ◆

A golf instructor once said, "If you aim at nothing, you'll hit it every time." It is not the intention of this chapter to draw clear lines anywhere that Scripture is not so clear. Our purpose is simply to suggest that a church that aims at nothing, or is confused as to the nature of its target, will inevitably suffer any number of potential ills.

The church will find itself mired in confusion about what is and is not appropriate church activity. The leaders of churches are constantly faced with a thousand voices, all clamoring for a slice of the church's time or finances. But without a clear understanding of the specific spheres of the church's responsibility, their decisions regarding giving will always be based upon whim rather than wisdom.

Some churches suffer from a truncated ministry where a pastor's "pet passions" set their agenda. The pastor might very well be a visionary who "has a heart" for this or that area of God's Kingdom. However, the Christian sphere of activity is always going to be larger than one man's present passion. The church may be doing one thing well, but what have they neglected in the process?

Finally, and still worse, how many churches suffer from a "top heavy" organizational flow chart that dies the death of hopeless stagnation in endless committee structures? Who would dare to suggest that the American Church needs more bureaucracy than it presently has? In our day the kingdoms of this world remain sadly un-assailed by the people of God. The reason: they are too busy.

The distinction between the Church and the Kingdom and the accompanying focus on the marks of the Church are the main tools in the pastor's toolbox. They provide a desperately needed compass for the Church's vision and mission.

5

The Identity of the Church

"So you will be my people, and I will be your God."

~ The Book of Jeremiah

"Don't you miss the old days?"

"What do you mean?"

"Well, I think our church has lost some of its excitement. I keep thinking back to when we were just a fledgling church plant. We met at each other's houses. We studied together, we prayed together, we went through enormous sacrifices together to make things work. I just felt like we were more of a family back then."

"Hmmm, what do you think happened?"

"I don't know. It just seemed like back then we were more interested in each other. We used to spend all our time talking about Bible-study topics and living our faith out in our communities. Now all we talk about is nursery workers, building programs, and Sunday school curriculum. I just don't know who we are anymore."

Loss of identity is endemic today.

Without the mirror of objective truth, people are increasingly incapable of measuring themselves. The ancient Greeks admonished their students to "know thyself," albeit for pagan ends. But the heroes of today wear their shaky sense of self as a badge. Singer/songwriter Sheryl Crow wonders "why I'm a stranger in my own life."

We have all heard stories of people suffering from total amnesia—an absolute loss of personal identity. The victim is left numb, directionless, and without any reason to live.

A loss of identity within the Church, likewise, can be fatal to her faith and life. A Church with a clouded understanding of herself is bound to suffer from lifelessness, confusion, and apathy among her members.

How much more zealous God's Church must be to clarify her sense of self! How careful she must be to adopt the Lord's understanding of her rather than the shifting sands of public opinion! How eager God is to give His Church—and those gathered individuals who compose His local churches—His very own personality and identity.

The Latin root from which the word "identity" is derived is *idem*. The word is a pronoun meaning *same*. To say that you "identify" with someone is to say that in some sense you see a similarity between yourselves. As a member of Christ's church, the believer truly relates to Christ. His or her life is bound up with Christ's as Christ's is bound up in the believer's.

This is wonderful news, and this chapter will spell it out: (1) God, by His grace, identifies with His people; (2) God's people, by His grace, identify with Him; (3) God's people, by His grace, identify with each other in fellowship; and, finally, (4) God's people, because of His grace, identify with those outside the Church.

God Identifies with His People

These days, an interesting event occurs in the uniquely American courting ritual known as "dating" that constitutes a significant mile marker in many relationships. The "D.T.R.," as it is affectionately known, occurs when a couple has had enough dates together to wonder what is going on between them. This is the time to "Define The Relationship," hence D.T.R. for short.

Typically (and sadly), the conversation is no more profound than this: He says, "Well, we've gone out quite a few times now, and we've spent a lot of time around each other, and, well—I just wanted you to know that I only want to date you now."

"Really?" she beams, "well, I only want to date you, too!"

"Really?" he beams back.

Presto, the relationship is "defined," albeit anemically so.

The practice of "defining the relationship" occurs all the time. Individuals in relationship live by rules or guidelines, whether they are conscious of it or not. For instance,

- A child understands that when daddy or mommy says "no," it means much more than when little brother or sister says the same thing.
- When friendships are formed, both parties make subtle negotiations concerning what is and is not appropriate for the relationship.
- When a couple weds, the institution of marriage creates

the context for their future in a binding agreement.

This human tendency to contract quietly with each other is a direct result of our spiritual DNA. Relating to one another is innate. The need to understand the rules of relating is instinctive. As God's image bearers, humankind mirrors the desire of the Creator to be "with" His people. "I will be your God, and you will be my people," YAHWEH tells Israel.[1] "There will be definition between you and me."

Thus, in the Garden of Eden, God lays down the terms of His relationship with Adam using what theologians call a "covenant." God promises Adam that if he obeys His command not to eat of the Tree of the Knowledge of Good and Evil, then Adam and all his posterity will live forever in perfect fellowship with Him. However, if he disobeys, both he and all his children after him will suffer the pains of death and separation from God (cf. Rom. 5:12ff.).

Genesis 3 describes the cosmic car wreck of the Fall. Adam sins against God. God and mankind are infinitely estranged. But out of His sheer grace, God makes a new covenant with Adam, a covenant of grace. He promises the woman in Genesis 3:15 that from her offspring shall come a champion who will certainly and finally break the allegiance that Adam has forged between himself and the Devil. Two humanities result from God's covenant of grace, those who are in league with the Devil and those who are redeemed (or "bought back") by God—the Church.

But the language at the beginning of verse 15 is striking. God says, "*I* will . . ."

"I will put enmity between you and the woman," He says to the serpent.

God identifies with His people. He takes sides with them.

From this first story in the Bible all the fundamental elements of God's identification with the Church can be noted. The story creates a frame through which we can consider how God has "defined the relationship" with His Church.

God identifies by reconciling

First, God relates to His Church as reconciled enemies.

Before being drawn by the Holy Spirit in the Body of Christ, men and women are *enemies* of God. This point cannot be understated. The unbeliever harbors a suppressed animosity towards God. Romans 1:18ff. makes it clear that all people, even in their natural state, know that there is a God and that they owe Him allegiance. But, because they are first committed to their own independence, they do not want to acknowledge God's existence or relevance, much less love and serve Him.

But sadly, for most members in the pew, the memory of this enmity is long since lost as they take God's grace for granted. Sin is nothing more than maladjustment or misfortune, so grace is nothing more than a helpful corrective or a lucky break. Little wonder that, when the opportunity to sit under the public declaration that God has reconciled His people to Himself in Christ comes Sunday after Sunday, it is acknowledged with the expressive equivalent of a "ho hum."

When God's people gather, it is a momentous event. Through the

Church, God pronounces the end of hostilities and establishes an eternal "cease fire" for His people.

How, then, is it possible to view attendance at this great event—*Lord's* Day worship—as optional? The bride of Christ tragically views her participation in her marriage to her covenant Head as voluntary. Christians file in late to worship. They allow golf tee times, unfinished reports at work, children's soccer practices, and just plain fatigue to excuse absence at stated worship! John Sartelle, pastor of Independent Presbyterian Church in Memphis, Tennessee, once told his congregation, "You walk around day after day, breathing God's air, enjoying the health that *He* gave to you, and taking for granted the unnumbered blessings He anonymously grants you every hour. It is a poor man indeed who cannot get up on Sunday mornings and *worship!*"

God identifies by mediating

Second, God identifies with the Church as a mediator.

The passage in Genesis 3 says that "he shall crush" the head of the serpent. This was God's business. God would take care of this cosmic matter. Mankind is not allowed to be creative in his approach to this God. He has ordained how His people will return to Him.

The way God determined to handle sin and Satan was through the mediating work of His Son, who would crush Satan's head.

Therefore, when the Church gathers, they do so only in union with the Lord Jesus Christ, the Church's champion. Ephesians 1:23 says that the Church is Jesus' "body, which is the fullness of Him who fills everything in every way."

Many commentators have wrestled with the referent of the "fullness" in verse 23. Is the Lord the fullness of the Church, or is the Church the fullness of the Lord? John Calvin takes the latter view, expressing the idea with staggering implications:

> By this word "fullness" he means that our Lord Jesus Christ and even God his Father account themselves imperfect, unless we are joined to him . . . as if a father should say, My house seems empty to me when I do not see my child in it. A husband will say, "I seem to be only half a man when my wife is not with me." After the same manner God says that he does not consider himself full and perfect, except by gathering us to himself and by making us all one with himself.[2]

How amazing! Of course, Calvin does not mean to suggest that there is any lack in God or Christ in any ultimate sense. However, this does not keep the passage from being startling. The Church in some *penultimate* sense *completes* the Godhead.

Believers, as the family of God by virtue of their being joined to Christ, participate in the very life of the Trinity.

How much more strongly can it be said? God identifies Himself so intimately with his people that He dares suggest that His happiness is wrapped up in the happiness of His people. All parents, as they stand over the crib of their newborn child, have an unspoken sense that they will never be happy again without the happiness of the little one. When the child succeeds, in a real sense, the parents succeed. When he fails, in a real sense, the parents hurt worse than the child. Behold the intimacy with which the God of the universe identifies with His children.

God's People Identify with Him

Martyn Lloyd-Jones, in his commentary on Ephesians 1:23, says that of the benefits derived from the Church's identification with Christ, "One of the most glorious is that in view of the fact that the Church is the body of Christ, and that He is the Head, we are entitled to say that *what is true of Him is true of us.*"[3]

Think of a body. Whatever happens to Christ, as the Head of the body, ultimately happens to the whole body. You cannot divorce one part of the body from another.

Paul even goes so far as to say, "For to me to live *is* Christ."[4]

If Christ is crucified, then His Church is crucified with Him. If Christ is raised, then His Church is raised with Him. If Christ is glorified, then His Church will be glorified with Him. Says Lloyd-Jones,

> Whatever the Head does the whole body does also. So we have been "crucified with Christ." When he was crucified I was crucified; my old man, the man I was in Adam, was crucified. I, the man that was born in sin, have died with Christ. In that

sense I am as dead as He was. I am "dead to sin," I am "dead to the law." I have finished with both. Crucified with Him, dead with Him, buried with Him! But, glorious fact, the thing the Apostle emphasizes is that I am also risen with Him. Even as the power of God raised Christ from the dead, He also raised me with Him.[5]

This is truly the lifeblood of the Church. To identify with Christ is to realize that He did not merely die to save His people from their sin, but He died to save His people from *themselves*. On the Cross, Jesus bears our entire identity. How rarely we grasp the magnitude of this claim.

Ask the average Christian why he believes he is right with God, and the inevitable response is, "Because Jesus died for my sin." But if this is all that has been accomplished on our behalf, then our redemption is only half accomplished. Christ did not merely die to take away punishment, but He also lived to give His life.

The implications of this go straight to the heart of what it means to be joined to Christ. If all Christ did was bring forgiveness, then, once the believer has received that forgiveness, he goes back on the treadmill. He may have "gotten off" once, but after that he goes back on probation. Therefore, the believer keeps feeling in and out of fellowship with God. He is deeply insecure, thinking somehow that his standing before God is still dependent upon *him*.

In our day, we have created a category within altar calls heretofore unheard of in the Bible (and church history, for that matter), known as the "rededication," to give hope to those who feel out of fellowship with God. But the Bible knows no such category. Being secure in Jesus' work has little to do with the quality (or lack thereof) of an individual's "dedication" to Jesus. It has everything to do with the quality of Jesus' astounding dedication to His child.

True Christian joy is a result of knowing that, because of the work of Christ, I am put beyond probation. God sees what Christ has done when he sees you just as He saw *your* sin when He looked upon His Son on the Cross. John Stott, in his book *The Cross of Christ*, says, "The essence of sin is man substituting himself for God, while the essence of salvation is God substituting himself for man."

As the Church gathers, she does so in union with her betrothed Husband, Jesus. Therefore, Paul can direct the Colossian believers to

> Let the peace of Christ rule in your hearts, since as members of one body you were called to peace. And be thankful. Let the word of Christ dwell in you richly as you teach and admonish one another with all wisdom, and as you sing psalms, hymns and spiritual songs with gratitude in your hearts to God. And whatever you do, whether in word or deed, do it all in the name of the Lord Jesus, giving thanks to God the Father through him. (3:15-17)

When believers sit side by side in a service of worship, their most fundamental common bond is their union with Christ. They have been "called to peace." They are united in their desire to come hear the "word of Christ" and to see that it dwells in them "richly." They are responsible to each other. They must "teach and admonish one another." They find that they rejoice together as well, singing "psalms, hymns, and spiritual songs" as they overflow with gratitude to God. They come to dine with Christ. At the Lord's Supper, which He directed His people to observe (Matt. 26:26ff.), believers meet with Christ to feed upon Him spiritually by faith. Little wonder, then, that the first Christians "devoted themselves to the apostles' teaching and to the fellowship, to the breaking of bread and to prayer" (Acts 2:42). These are "standard operating procedures" for the Church as she identifies with her Lord.

How many times has this refrain been heard on the way out of Sunday morning service? "Well, I guess today was okay, but I just didn't really get anything out of the service today." But this comment betrays the true motive for attending in the first place. They act as if the service was *for them*. It is not. The reason believers gather is because they are infatuated with their Lord. They gather because they owe Him their lives, their duty, and their devotion. The question has nothing to do with whether or not we get anything out of a particular service of worship. The question is, "Did *He* get anything out of us?"

God's People Identify with Each Other

Recently, a friend returned from hiking the entire Appalachian Trail. From Mount Katahdin in Maine to Springer Mountain in Georgia, the Appalachian National Scenic Trail wanders the ridges and valleys of the Appalachian range for 2,167 miles. It took him six and a half months to walk. There were far too many experiences and adventures to relate in the short time we spoke when he returned; but when I asked about the part of his trip that stood out to him the most, his answer was surprising.

"That's easy. The Trail community," he said. "There is literally no way that you could complete a two-thousand-mile hike over half a year by yourself. On the trail you join up with literally hundreds of other hikers who all have the same goal in view, finishing the Trail. And the sense of community was so rich. Everyone helped everyone. If a group of people found out that you were a 'through hiker' they went out of their way to give you food, shelter, clothing, whatever you needed. Though these people weren't necessarily Christians, I learned more about what it means to be connected to people than I have ever learned in my life."

In some ways, it ought to be embarrassing to modern evangelicals that our culture screams so loudly for community. The self-help book section in most bookstores is packed with reading to help people feel "connected." We long to know what it means to be in real, genuine fellowship with one another. Because we are created in the image of God, we long to be in relationship with one another, but our sin creates the opposite urge.

Who cannot relate to the longing that exists in each of us to be truly and deeply known? The desire for a relationship of utter transparency where another person sees us in all of our flaws and warts—and does not cringe at the sight—is at the heart of every man and woman. Yet, the very thought of having someone see us down to the bottom, as it were, is a terrifying prospect.

In Galatians 3:10, Paul explains that in our natural state, "under the law," we are "under a curse." Usually the word *curse* conjures up ideas of witches' brew and sorcery, but Paul is referring to the curse of the law that separates us from the one relationship we were built to enjoy. Because we are separated from *that* relationship, we experience alienation from each other as well, so that, when a man is born again, he is not just set right with God; he is also set right with those around him. Ephesians 2:14, 19 says, "He himself is our peace, who has made the two one and has destroyed the barrier, the dividing wall of hostility . . . Consequently, you are no longer foreigners and aliens, but *fellow citizens with God's people and members of God's household.*"[6]

The fundamental essence of the Church from an earthly point of view is the connection between people. The Church means that I must get along with you, and you must learn to put up with me, too.

The greatest challenge that a church faces as it grows is the temptation to view "Church" as the physical building in which believers meet. Though rarely explicitly stated, most believers equate "Church" with "bricks and mortar." But the Church is *not entailed* in a building. The identity of the Church rests in covenant relationships, believers who have bound themselves together under the common bond of being identified with Christ and vowing to serve Him. When believers gather, *there* is the Church.

The Church is a building only in the spiritual sense. True, believers are "living stones" with Christ as the "chief cornerstone." One friend said it this way, "The 'Church' basically binds me to love, sacrifice and serve you—regardless of what I think of you." This is the heart of true fellowship. The Body of Christ is called to love one another "as Christ loved the Church" (Eph. 5:25), to forgive one another as many times as the other repents (Matt. 18:21ff.), and to bear one another's burdens in the Lord (Gal. 6:2).

There are few more painful experiences in a church than the fall of one of her members into serious sin. However, it is equally tragic when the rest of the body reacts to the event as if they were living in an already-glorified church. We gasp and race to the phone to "share" the event with a close friend in order to "pray" for that one. Meanwhile, we savor the sin of gossip as the real morsel under our tongue.

No wonder the most common charge leveled by the watching world against the church is "hypocrisy." Who would want to be vulnerable with their struggles in a community that executes its wounded? But the Body of Christ ought to represent one of the most honest collections of people on Earth. Tragically, those who struggle the most with serious sin are often the loneliest.

Consequently, the radical work of Christ ought to create an environment of utter humility. "But for the grace of God, there go I" needs to be brought back into the Church's vernacular. High-mindedness and condescension to anyone ought to be a most feared sin.

All Christians have experienced the "hard to love" in a local congregation of saints. You may very well wonder if the body of worshiping believers to whom you are called to submit in the Lord has a sign posted at the front door reading, "Come unto me, all ye who are socially awkward." These people never seem to say the right things. They are constantly annoying you with their questions (or their "answers" if you have ever had a Sunday school class with them). They come over to your home at inconvenient times when you are desperately trying to get other things done. They call, sometimes night after night, wanting to talk about nothing but the most mundane and inane subjects.

However, in the face of so-called "impossible people", we see the Gospel lived out before our very eyes. Jesus warns us that at the last day believers will be judged on how they clothed Him, how they fed Him, how they came and visited Him when in prison. "I tell you the truth, whatever you did for one of the least of these brothers of mine, you did for me" (Matt. 25:40).

It is as if God were saying, "Until you learn to love this person, to put up with mind-numbing annoyances, to forgive him for the same sin over and over and over again, to invite him into your home even when he repulses you—until you learn to relate to this impossible person, you'll never know what it is like for me to relate to you."

Thank God for those hard to love. They are our mirrors.

The goal of the Church is not to pack people in Sunday after Sunday. It is not to offer programs that are more "dynamic" and "relevant" than the church down the street. It is not to provide a haven where Christian businessmen make their contacts for this week's sales goal. The goal of the Church is to rally believers around

the life-changing power of the gospel, making us transparent and con-
fident people who love one another and exist to meet one another's
needs as we glorify God.

The goal of the Church is to identify with one another as God has
identified with her.

God's People Identify with Humanity

Finally, the people of God live with an eye toward those who are
outside the family of faith.

The Church longs to speak to the world for the same reason that
a ten-year-old cannot wait to tell you about his new Sony Playstation 2.
He is enamored with it, he thinks about it when he is away from it,
and he cannot wait to tell you about the great new game he just
bought for it.

Likewise, the believer is infatuated with the gospel. Like the angels
in heaven, he longs to consider the truths that frame his salvation.
He talks about it for the same reason that he talks about the great
seven iron that he used to hit from 175 yards out on hole four yes-
terday at the Municipal Course. He is excited!

Most modern books on evangelism miss this point. Constant
efforts to systematize and program evangelism schemes often have
the opposite result of discouraging believers from sharing their faith.
Motivation for witnessing of God's grace narrows itself down to sheer
browbeating, guilt manipulation.

But the motivation for sharing the gospel ought to be embedded
in the message itself. The gospel does not just talk about the power

of God. Romans 1:16 says that the gospel *is* the power of God for salvation. Few "experts" on evangelism ever stop to consider that one of the reasons why people are not sharing their faith is because there is no "good news" in their "gospel." They do not talk about Christ to their co-workers because they do not have anything to say. Perhaps the first step in teaching on evangelism ought to be introducing people to the "evangel."

Proponents of evangelistic programs fall broadly into one of two categories. On the one hand, there are those who would advocate a bold, confrontational style of evangelism. Believers are encouraged to "step up!" "get out of the pews!" and "put the gospel into action!" On the other hand, so-called lifestyle evangelists would recommend a more relational approach to evangelism, preferring evangelistic encounters to grow out of naturally formed relationships. The "confrontational" people usually resent the "lifestyle" people because, in their view, they are only making excuses for their lack of boldness in witnessing. Meanwhile, the "lifestyle" people roll their eyes at the "confrontational" people because their approach ignores the relational dynamic of talking to people about their faith.

But surely this is a false dichotomy. A Christian who claims to have embraced the gospel but does not "put it into action" is no Christian at all. Jesus is Lord over every area of the believer's life so that every encounter he has is potentially an encounter for the gospel. Yet all encounters have a relational element to them. Our relationship may be one of long-time friends or of first-time acquaintances, but some kind of relationship is inevitable.

So if the Church is to recognize the responsibility to bear her identity before the watching world, she must rethink a Church-centered approach to evangelism. The voice of the Puritans can shed much light here. J. I. Packer, in his work on the Puritans entitled *The Quest for Godliness: The Puritan Vision of the Christian Life,* describes their view of evangelism this way:

> The Puritan practitioners of evangelism were pastors with captive audiences (for church-going was part of national life in those days), and their evangelizing of those who sat regularly in the pews was to the pastors no more, just as it was no less, than a main part of their larger task of building up the whole congregation in Christ. Their program as evangelists was no more specialized than this: *to teach and apply the Scriptures in a patient, thorough way, ranging wide in their declarations of the whole counsel of God,* but constantly returning to three themes. Theme one was the length, breadth, height and depth of everyone's need to be converted and saved. Theme two was the length, breadth, depth and height of the love of God, who sent his Son to the cross for sinners, and of Christ, who from his throne calls burdened souls to himself for their salvation. Theme three was the ups, downs, blockages and pitfalls that face us as we travel the road from

ignorant complacency about our spiritual state to informed, self-despairing, clear-headed and whole-hearted faith in Christ.[7]

It might very well be objected that this view represents an antiquated notion of evangelism, for Packer himself admits that "churchgoing was a part of national life in those days." In our day, churchgoing has ceased to be a part of the average person's week. However, this is only true if "Church" is confined to what happens in a particular building. The goal of evangelism in the Church ought to be to create an environment where "evangelism" is the air that Christians breathe.

Will Metzger, in his book *Tell The Truth*, laments that most evangelism today seems to operate under the theme "the least amount of truth, for the most amount of people."[8] Evangelism is pared down to the momentary encounter where limited exposure to basic truths of the gospel is exchanged for the whole counsel of God. However, this is a truncated view of the Church's mission. True evangelism ought to be, as Metzger says, that which seeks to get the *most* amount of truth to the *most* amount of people. "But you can't present the 'whole counsel of God' to someone in one encounter," many object.[9]

Perhaps not, but believers can make it their goal to place people in direct contact with the freight train of the Word of God, both in their own conversation and in the organized preaching and teaching of the Word at their local church. The identity of the Church is marked by a commitment to provide as many people as possible with as much exposure as possible to the patient, faithful exposition of the whole counsel of God in the Scriptures.

Ringing throughout this whole discussion ought to be the question of motivation. Are the relationships that I have projects or people? Am I involved in the lives of others (even under the guise of evangelism) so that I can feel better about myself when they "make a decision for Christ" or "pray a prayer of acceptance?" Or am I learning to love *individuals* sacrificially who are unique in their station in life and their readiness to hear spiritual things? Treating people as projects too often excuses an attempt to avoid the messy, day-in, day-out struggles of learning to confront myself in the lives of others for the sake of the message of the gospel.

The Church is nothing if it lacks a sense of identity. The real fact is: The church without an identity is not the Church at all. It is not the Church of God Almighty. It is a shadow. It is a sham.

God has identified with a certain people, His Church. God's people, by God's grace, will identify with Him. God's people, as they identify with Him, will identify with each other. Out of the life of the Church in fellowship, it then moves to identify with the world.

The Church loses its vitality and passion when it enters a time of identity crisis. To forget to keep "first things first" is the quickest way to suck the life out of a congregation of often well-intentioned believers.

The good news is that a true church will never completely stray. When the Word is held up as the only rule of faith and practice, the *sufficient* Word of God for mankind, the Lord's Supper is seen and celebrated, and believers covenant together to be about the difficult, frustrating, soul-straining task of loving one another—then, the Church will maintain a soul-nourishing identity that her Lord intended for her to have.

6

The Submission of the Church

"Then Jesus came to them and said, 'All authority in heaven and on earth has been given to me.'"

~The Gospel of Matthew

"When I fight authority, authority always wins."

~John Cougar Mellencamp

On a May morning in 1685,[1] a Scottish woman named Margaret Wilson was bound to a wooden stake that stood in the bed of the Blednoch Burn (a local river). She was about to undergo execution by drowning. Her charge? She was what was known as a "Covenanter," a Scot who held to the supreme authority of God's Word and to the headship of Christ alone (rather than the British monarch) over the Church.

As the tide began to come in, and the waters around her began to rise, Margaret sang a psalm she knew by heart, and then read from a copy of the Bible that she still had on her person. She chose to read from the eighth chapter of the Book of Romans. Before long, the frigid water began to run over her. Soldiers nearby grabbed her, forcing her out of the water enough to gasp for air, and demanded that she pray for the king, "as he is supreme over all persons and causes, ecclesiastic as well as civil." Since she refused to believe that anyone but Christ was the head of the Church, she prayed with her remaining strength that God would grant salvation to the king. One officer, furious at her refusal, cursed at her and demanded she recite oaths denying her views. When she would not, she was forced back into the cold river, where she drowned.

She was eighteen years old.

Submission to Jesus' Lordship

Margaret's bravery is clearly evident, but should she have died over something so insignificant as who is the head of the Church? Be careful not to miss the lesson that church history holds for us. As believers at the beginning of the 21st century, we are strong on pragmatism (i.e., doing what works), and weak on principled thinking about the Church. We might do well to remember that there are those who have gone before us who literally died for their convictions about Church authority.

Does the Bible warrant such zeal regarding Christ's authority over His Church?

When the Scriptures speak about the headship of Jesus Christ over His Church, they pull no punches. Consider these examples:

> **Ephesians 1:20b–22:** "[God] raised him from the dead and seated him at his right hand in the heavenly realms, far above all rule and authority,

power and dominion, and every title that can be given, not only in the present age but also in the one to come. And God placed all things under his feet and appointed him to be head over everything for the church, which is his body, the fullness of him who fills everything in every way."

Philippians 2:9–11: "Therefore God exalted him to the highest place and gave him the name that is above every name, that at the name of Jesus every knee should bow, in heaven and on earth and under the earth, and every tongue confess that Jesus Christ is Lord, to the glory of God the Father."

Colossians 1:18: "And he is the head of the body, the church; he is the beginning and the first-born from among the dead, so that in everything he might have the supremacy."

Such language leaves little room for doubt about Christ's absolute authority over the Church, as well as everything else. How, though, does that tangibly express itself in the goings-on of a believer's life? After all, Christ is no longer physically present for us to appear before Him.

One of the great scholarly works of Christian literature that takes up the subject of the Church is by James Bannerman, a Scottish the-ologian of the nineteenth century. Entitled *The Church of Christ,* it provides this description of how societies of people operate:

> It is essential to every society of a regular and orderly kind, to have *office-bearers* to represent the mind of the community, to conduct its business, and to act on its behalf . . . Second, it must have its *laws,* to bind both members and office-bearers, to regulate their conduct in reference to each other and to foreign parties, and to determine the course and order of their transactions as a society.[2]

According to Bannerman, this holds true for the Church as well. Christ is indeed the head of the Church and, therefore, of each local church. Thus, Christ's headship is recognized in the local church when the people of God submit to His Word and His leaders. But what does this actually involve?

Submission to Jesus' Word

When Moses recorded the travels of the people of Israel in the wilderness, he provided us with an interesting perspective on what determined the people's movements from place to place.

> Whenever the cloud lifted from above the Tent, the Israelites set out; wherever the cloud settled, the Israelites encamped. *At the Lord's command* the Israelites set out, and *at his command* they

encamped. As long as the cloud stayed over the tabernacle, they remained in camp. When the cloud remained over the tabernacle a long time, the Israelites obeyed the *Lord's order* and did not set out. Sometimes the cloud was over the tabernacle only a few days; *at the Lord's command* they would encamp, and then *at his command* they would set out . . . *At the Lord's command they encamped, and at the Lord's command they set out.* They obeyed the *Lord's order,* in accordance with his command through Moses.[3]

Do you get the sneaking suspicion that Moses is making a point here?

Today, God's people are in no less need of following His lead in their journey together. The Israelites were led through the wilderness by the cloud; God's people are now led by the Scriptures, His authoritative Word. If it is indeed true that "man does not live on bread alone, but on every word that comes from the mouth of God" (Deut. 8:3; Matt. 4:4), then the Bible must be *the* authority for not only the Church at large, but for each local church as well.

But what does this look like in practice? Many churches would be quick to assert, "We take our cues from Scripture." But actually doing so will radically affect a local church. What would we expect to find in a church where the shock waves of God's own words have reverberated?

Centrality of Scripture in worship

First, the Scriptures would inform every aspect of a church's meetings of worship. From the call to worship at the beginning of the service to the benediction at the end, everything would derive its content and meaning from the Word of God.

Prayer would be marked by biblical content and biblical priorities. The sorts of hymns and songs sung would convey both simple truths (as do the Scriptures) and profound theological insights (as do the Scriptures).

Monetary gifts would go toward individuals and ministries pursuing biblical aims, particularly the spread of the gospel by word and deed.

The sacraments would be administered in accord with the Scriptures, and overall, the service would be marked by a biblical sense of order and reverence (1 Cor. 14:40).

But perhaps the most telltale sign of all would occur when the sermon took place. We would expect to hear sermons upon the Scriptures themselves in which the preacher would read and direct the worshipers' attention to the text, explain the text, and apply it to the lives of those sitting before him. Over time, we would expect the preacher to draw upon passages throughout the entirety of Scripture, perhaps preaching through entire books of the Bible.

This means the pastor would have to fight the temptation to avoid difficult passages inevitably encountered as he made his way through the whole of Scripture. He would have to fight the temptation merely to skip from verse to verse and passage to passage, preaching only on those topics he most enjoyed or that seemed most "relevant." He would have to fight the temptation to *read into* the passage what he wanted it to say, or to *launch from* the passage onto a personal soapbox, rather than *derive from* the passage what it actually said. He might even have to fight the temptation to abuse the use of illustrations, using them to manipulate listeners rather than to shed light on the passage at hand.

But there would be one other essential aspect to the sermon.

As the Word of God was opened, explained, and applied, we would hear the good news of who Jesus Christ is and what He has done on behalf of His people. The Bible is a rather large book, written over hundreds and hundreds of years, with multiple contributors. Yet, it ultimately has one Author, and it ultimately conveys one great story—that "God so loved the world that he gave his one and only Son, that whoever believes in him shall not perish but have eternal life" (John 3:16).

By reading the four Gospels, it becomes clear that Jesus views the Scriptures as a body of material about *Himself.*

- To the Jews that doubted Him, we find Him saying, "You diligently study the Scriptures because you think that by them you possess eternal life. These are the Scriptures that testify about me" (John 5:39).
- To the two disciples that He joined on the road to Emmaus, Luke records that "beginning with Moses and all the Prophets, he explained to them what was said in all the Scriptures concerning himself" (Luke 24:27).

With this in mind, we would expect to hear preaching and teach-

ing that was wide in its scope, but always *Christ-centered in its focus.*
Paul, the preacher, made this point quite clear when he wrote to a
church: "I resolved to know nothing while I was with you except
Jesus Christ and him crucified" (1 Cor. 2:2).

Centrality of Scripture in thinking

Typically, when we talk about the Christian life, we begin with
what we are to *do.* That is not the starting point of Scripture, however.
In his *magnum opus,* when Paul makes the great transition from the
doctrine of the gospel to its implications for the lives of Christians,
he writes: "Do not conform any longer to the pattern of this world,
but be transformed by the renewing of *your mind.* Then you will be
able to test and approve what God's will is–his good, pleasing and
perfect will" (Rom. 12:2).[4] (It is noteworthy that most of the New
Testament epistles more or less follow this format; they begin with a
section that emphasizes doctrine–how we are to think–and *then* pro-
ceed with an emphasis on application–how we are to live.)
Elsewhere, Paul records this prayer that he and Timothy regularly
offered on behalf of the church in the city of Colosse:

> For this reason, since the day we heard about
> you, we have not stopped praying for you and ask-
> ing God to fill you with *the knowledge of his will
> through all spiritual wisdom and understanding. And we
> pray this in order that you may live a life worthy of the
> Lord and may please him in every way:* bearing fruit in

every good work, growing in the knowledge of God, being strengthened with all power according to his glorious might so that you may have great endurance and patience, and joyfully giving thanks to the Father, who has qualified you to share in the inheritance of the saints in the kingdom of light.[5]

What a list! Would not every Christian want to see the lives of fellow church members marked by fruitfulness, powerful strength over the long haul and an overwhelming sense of thankfulness to God? Of course, but what is the means by which Paul and Timothy prayed this would happen? They prayed for a profound change in *thinking* that would lead to a profound change in *living.* Apparently, believers are changed from the inside out as their thinking changes.

Someone might read this, though, and think, "That sounds so dogmatic–I just want to live a Spirit-filled life." A desire to live a Spirit-filled life is commendable, but again, what would that look like in practice? Interestingly, when the Holy Spirit was poured out at Pentecost, and approximately three thousand men and women were converted through Peter's preaching, what is the first thing we learn about the subsequent lives of these Spirit-filled believers? Luke points out that they "devoted themselves to the apostles' *teaching*" (Acts 2:42).[6] That is to say, these new Christians did not merely rush headlong into Christian activity, but they began with a devoted pursuit of truth through the (sometimes difficult!) teaching of the apostles.

Therefore, to bring our focus back to the local church, we would expect that, where a church claimed to be submissive to the Word of God, its day-to-day life and decision-making would be driven by biblical thinking rather than by something else. What else might drive a church's activity? The answer is, practically anything.[7] For instance, a few years ago, one church decided that it was going to take some proactive steps to build its numbers. To accomplish this, the pastor urged that a particular approach to child rearing become the church's new "niche" in the community. This approach would not only include broad biblical principles about child-rearing (e.g., leading by godly example, the necessity of biblical discipline, etc.), but it would also provide particulars about such matters as a baby's sleeping and feeding schedules. Not surprisingly, the plan did not achieve what the pastor had hoped. Even if it had, though, what is the real problem here? The real problem is that such an emphasis has nothing to do with the real "niche" of a local church (see chapter four), as defined in the Scriptures. Sadly, the pastor pursued a course of action that was inconsistent with, and could have been stopped by, a good dose of biblical reflection.

There are countless substitutes for scriptural thinking in a church's life, but perhaps the most common substitute is *expediency*. One dictionary defines what is expedient as that which is "useful for effecting a desired result; convenient." This could take a number of forms. For instance, expediency in local churches often takes the form of *doing what worked somewhere else*. A church (usually one that was small and has now become large) adopts a particular technique or develops a program, and soon the people in that church's area are beating a path to the church's door. As word spreads about the numeric success generated by this church's approach, other churches begin to take the same course of action with hopes that they will see the same sort of numeric response. Some do, others do not. Again, though, what is the real issue? The real issue is whether this technique or program is the end product of biblical thinking. Does it prioritize what Scripture prioritizes, and convey what Scripture conveys, or is it an approach in which the end (generating and keeping new members) justifies the means? Does the approach merely appeal to the target audience's felt needs, or does the church place greater emphasis upon the profound needs of human hearts, needs that might go *unfelt*? We could summarize, then, by asking this question: *Is this church's activity driven by theology, or by methodology?* Does this church know—biblically speaking—why it does what it does?

Submission to Jesus' Chosen Leaders

Christ not only executes His authority through His Word, but through His leaders as well. In fact, the two are forever linked. Since Christ alone has all authority, and since He has authoritatively provided all that His people need in His Word, any authority that church leaders possess must be derived from the Scriptures alone. One theologian put it this way:

> Christ is the church's only King and Head; and
> this implies that its affairs must be regulated by His
> mind and will revealed in His word. . . . The office-

bearers of the church are not lords over God's heritage: they have no dominion over men's faith; they have no jurisdiction over the conscience; they are the mere interpreters of Christ's word, the mere administrators of the laws that He has enacted.[8]

But *who* are these leaders, and what God-given authority do they actually have?

Chosen local leaders

First, we need to define what we mean by "church leaders." These are the men in a local church who are alternately referred to in the New Testament as "elders," "overseers," and "shepherds" (some older translations also used the words "presbyters" for elders, and "bishops" for overseers). The fact that these alternate titles refer to the same type of church leader can be demonstrated by comparing several passages.

> **Acts 20:17, 28:** "From Miletus, Paul sent to Ephesus for the *elders* of the Church." [Later, Paul addresses this same group of elders.] "'Keep watch over yourselves and all the flock of which the Holy Spirit has made you *overseers*. Be *shepherds* of the church of God, which he bought with his own blood.'"

> **Titus 1:5–7a:** "The reason I left you in Crete was

that you might straighten out what was left unfinished and appoint *elders* in every town, as I directed you. An elder must be blameless, the husband of but one wife, a man whose children believe and are not open to the charge of being wild and disobedient. Since an *overseer* is entrusted with God's work, he must be blameless—"

1 Peter 5:1–2a: "To the *elders* among you, I appeal as a fellow *elder,* a witness of Christ's sufferings and one who also will share in the glory to be revealed: Be *shepherds* of God's flock that is under your care, serving as *overseers.*" [9]

The matter may seem academic to some readers, but it is very significant for how we think about the local church. Elder, overseer, and shepherd describe the same New Testament church office. [10]

A plurality of chosen local leaders

Second, we need to take note of a pattern in the Scriptures that occurs too often to be ignored. When we see the presence of a local church in the New Testament, we do not see just one elder at the helm. Rather, we see a *plurality of elders* in each local church. Again, this is demonstrated by considering several passages.

Acts 14:23: "Paul and Barnabas appointed *elders* for them *in each church* and, with prayer and fasting, committed them to the Lord, in whom they had put their trust."

Acts 20:17: "From Miletus, Paul sent to Ephesus for the *elders of the church.*"

Philippians 1:1: "Paul and Timothy, servants of Christ Jesus, to all the saints in Christ Jesus at Philippi, together with the *overseers* and deacons."

Titus 1:5: "The reason I left you in Crete was that you might straighten out what was left unfinished and appoint *elders in every town,* as I directed you."

James 5:14: "Is any one of you sick? He should call the *elders of the church* to pray over him and anoint him with oil in the name of the Lord."[11]

Why is this so important? Because the New Testament is clear that an elder is not to run a one-man show in a local church setting. There is to be a plurality of elders present (numbers will vary with the size of a church), who exercise their God-given authority *in a group capacity, not an individual one.* Therefore, when we speak of submitting to church leaders, what we have in mind is submission to the authority that elders possess in their group capacity.

Local authority

But, is speaking of the power of these leaders as "authoritative" too strong a statement? After all, did we not begin with the assertion that Christ is the only head of the Church? Yes, but a means by which Christ exercises His authority over the Church is the authority entrusted to these church leaders.

If we are uncomfortable with the language of "submitting to" or "obeying" church leaders, the Scriptures are not. Though mentioned earlier, Hebrews 13:17 should be remembered: *"Obey* your leaders and *submit* to their authority. They keep watch over you as men who must give an account. *Obey* them so that their work will be a joy, not a burden, for that would be of no advantage to you." Other passages seem to echo the same thought.

- "The elders who direct the affairs of the church well are worthy of double honor, especially those whose work is preaching and teaching" (1 Tim. 5:17).
- "Now we ask you, brothers, to respect those who work hard among you, who are over you in the Lord and who admonish you. Hold them in the highest regard in love because of their work" (1 Thess. 5:12–13a).

What does this mean for the church member in the pews? It means that, though perhaps a difficult truth to embrace, the elders have a God-given authority in regard to a member's spiritual oversight, and this authority is to be received with a submissive and willing attitude. Simply put, it means that the decisions of the elders are not mere suggestions; they are something to be obeyed.

Regional authority

What happens, though, when a matter arises that affects more than one particular gathering of believers? This is a fitting question, since the word *church* in the New Testament is not limited to the entire body of Christ, nor is it limited to local congregations. Sometimes it is used of all the Christians in a particular region. For instance, Luke could speak of "the church at Jerusalem" (Acts 8:1), and given the numeric growth that had taken place up to that point, it seems virtually impossible that this could refer to one single congregation of Christians. Later, he refers to "the church throughout Judea, Galilee, and Samaria" (Acts 9:31). How would questions pertaining to a regional "church" be decided, and how binding would such decisions be?

A fascinating example of this occurs in the fifteenth chapter of Acts. The context is that the early church was experiencing rapid growth, and many of the new converts were Gentiles (non-Jews). Since Gentiles generally had not undergone circumcision, some professing believers were teaching these new converts in Antioch, "Unless you are circumcised, according to the custom taught by Moses, you cannot be saved" (vv. 1, 5). Paul and Barnabas took the polar opposite viewpoint, which created a dispute. The verdict would have ramifications for the life of the entire Church.

But who would render the crucial decision? As it turned out, an assembly was convened in Jerusalem, composed of "the apostles and the elders" (vv. 6, 22). That is to say, the assembly was composed of not only the apostles (*the* leaders of the early church), but also of elders from throughout the region affected by the future decision. It is worth noting that, during the course of this assembly's meeting, the apostles never cut the discussion short by rendering a supernatural, infallible decision. The Scriptures were considered, discussion took place, and a decision was reached. Other members of the early church were apparently present as well (see vv. 12, 22), but when the final decision was rendered, it came from "the apostles and elders."

The assembly concluded that the Gentiles were *not* required to undergo circumcision, and they drafted a letter to express their conclusion, which was to be carried by Paul and Barnabas (along with other representatives of the assembly) back to Antioch. What is especially relevant is how this letter begins. It reads: "The apostles and elders, your brothers, to the Gentile believers in Antioch, Syria and Cilicia: Greetings. We have heard that some went out from us *without our authorization* and disturbed you, troubling your minds by what they said" (vv. 23–24).[12]

The word that is used by the assembly for their "authorization" is the Greek verb *diastello.* The reason this choice of words is so interesting is that is conveys the thought of a command, not merely permission. Several times in the Gospel of Mark it is used of Jesus when He commanded His followers not to reveal who He was. For instance, in the ninth chapter of Mark, after Jesus was transfigured before Peter, James, and John, we read this: "As they were coming down the mountain, Jesus *gave them orders* not to tell anyone what they had seen until the Son of Man had risen from the dead" (v. 9).[13] Elsewhere, in the Book of Hebrews, the same verb is used to describe a command given by God from Mount Sinai (12:20). One standard theological reference work says of this verb's usage in the Septuagint[14] that "the ref[erence] is always to the precise, irrevocable and definitive directions of God and declarations of his will." This same work goes on to say that, when we encounter this verb in the assembly's letter in Acts 15, "the reference is not to a commission but to strict orders."[15] The assembly was in effect saying to the Gentile believers, "We did not command these teachers to go out and teach what they are teaching, so disregard what they told you."

So what? Actually, the implications of this may be quite massive for each of our lives, but we must also be careful here.

When we study a biblical narrative (that is, a historical episode like the one in Acts 15), we must exercise caution not to equate the record of an event with a command from God for us to do the same thing. In other words, just because an action is *reported* in Scripture does not mean that it is *commanded* in Scripture. For instance, in the eleventh chapter of the Book of Judges, a man named Jephthah vowed that if the Lord gave him victory in his warfare against the Ammonites, he would sacrifice whatever came out the door of his home when he returned home. (Bad idea.) As it turned out, his *daughter* was the first one out the door! The chapter ends with the record that "he did to her as he had vowed." Obviously, this is *not* something God commands His people to do; yet it is reported as a truthful account of the events.

On the other hand, sometimes a biblical narrative reports an action and sets it forth in a positive light. That is to say, it is both reported and *commended,* though not directly commanded. For instance, in the nineteenth chapter of Luke, when the tax collector Zacchaeus is changed by his encounter with Jesus, he responds, "Look, Lord! Here and now I give half of my possessions to the poor, and if I have cheated anybody out of anything, I will pay him back four times the amount" (v. 8). Old Testament law required repayment to offended parties, but Zacchaeus' response exceeds even the requirements of the law. Is this passage a command for all those who have fallen into financial corruption to do the same? No, but the decision of Zacchaeus is recorded as a commendable response to the grace of God in his life.

Why is this relevant to our consideration of church leaders? It is relevant because we do not want to go beyond what is clearly *commanded* in the Scriptures, yet we want to be aware of what is *commended* in the Scriptures, as well. We are *commanded* in the Scriptures to submit to church leaders, as we noted above. On the other hand, we should remember that there are no explicit commands in the Bible that each local church must have a plurality of elders. However, this practice is reported on numerous occasions in the New Testament, and by all accounts it was a practice done with the approval and participation of the apostles. Similarly, there is no explicit command that the elders of a particular region or country meet regularly to consider matters that affect the life of the Church at large. Yet, we should also remember that on at least one occasion, the apostles and elders met as a gathered assembly to consider a defining issue that the Church was facing. Furthermore, when they drafted an official response to the issue, they indicated that they had the God-given authority to determine who should go out teaching the gospel and who should not. These things were done with the approval of the apostles, and they are commended (though not commanded) in the Word of God.

Implications of leaders' rule for today's Church

So how does this affect Christians in our own day? To begin with, there are literally thousands of church denominations in the United States, but the number of organizations, agencies, and ministries that engage in biblical teaching is a greater number by far. When a believer stops and considers this staggering number, he may experience a feeling of being torn between two convictions. On the one hand, he rejoices that more and more people are given access to the gospel of Jesus Christ that all of us so desperately need. As Paul was able to say, "The important thing is that in every way, whether from false motive or true, Christ is preached. And because of this I rejoice" (Phil. 1:18). On the other hand, there is also the realization that with increased levels of teaching come increased likelihood of error. To put it quite simply, people can think that they are teaching the gospel and getting it right, but they can be getting it very wrong.

If this is the case, it forces us to ask a question: Who is to be the God-given check on misinterpretations of the Bible, particularly when the doctrine of salvation is misunderstood? If several groups or ministries are using the same Bible and arriving at different conclusions, even about matters that lie at the heart of the gospel, who is to say which view is correct and which ones are false?

Having considered the passages cited above, we can respond by saying this: *the New Testament* **commends** *the view that biblical teaching in a church or area should find some expression of accountability to the elders in that church or area.* If the ministry of the Word of God is the unique work of the Church (again, see chapter four), and if the Church-at-large finds local expression in the local church, and if the elders are the God-given leaders of each local church, then this conclusion makes sense.

It is difficult to overstate the implications of this. Imagine for a moment how the landscape of 21st-century Christianity would change if everyone who wanted to engage in biblical teaching were *not* allowed to do so! Imagine, rather, that all who desired to do such teaching saw the wisdom of expressing their intentions to their church leaders, as well as conveying some idea of what the content of their teaching would be. Then, consider what this would do—over time—to the church leaders themselves. As they repeatedly faced requests for approval of teaching, but as they were confronted with inconsistent views of biblical truth and even the gospel itself, they would be forced to return again and again to Scripture to hone their understanding of sound doctrine.[16] False teachers—however well-meaning—would not be endorsed and sent out by the church leaders, and they would be exhorted to reexamine their views. Sound teachers would be encouraged that they were indeed teaching "the truth that is in Jesus" (Eph. 4:21). This would be nothing short of—revolutionary.

Needless to say, this will sound utterly unrealistic to some. But the question before us is not so much how we will single-handedly reform all of Christendom. The question before us involves what *our* view is of the leaders God had placed over us in the local church. Are they men through whom the Lord Jesus Christ exercises His loving authority over me, or are they merely another set of people in my life whom I critique, then ignore? The way we answer these questions will communicate what we *really* believe about the headship of Jesus Christ over His Church.

7

The Love of the Church

"Live a life of love, just as Christ loved us and gave himself up for us as a fragrant offering and sacrifice to God."

~The Epistle to the Ephesians

"To give a love, you gotta live a love. To live a love, you
gotta be 'part of.'"

~Neil Young

You have seen it before. The bride and groom stand virtually inches
apart, holding hands, and they make vows to love one another in a
way that they have never loved anyone else. Perhaps you have heard
this very wording:

> I take you to be my wedded wife/husband,
> to have and to hold from this day forward;
> for better, for worse,
> for richer, for poorer,
> in sickness and in health,
> to love and to cherish
> till death us do part,

according to God's holy law;

and this is my solemn vow.

But what does loving someone in this way *really* involve? What does it look like to keep such vows?

Perhaps if we asked the brand new husband–commanded in Scripture to love his wife as Christ loves the Church–he would respond, "It means that I would lay down my life for my wife." This is a noble response, but statistically, the opportunity to do so will probably never occur. As one wife concluded in an article entitled "Husbands, Forget the Heroics!": "Most women do not want their men to die for them. They want their men to live for them."[1]

Her words underscore a simple truth: *love is never a mere abstraction.* Love finds expression in particular, day-to-day actions.

In the authors' denomination, several questions are administered to those wishing to become members of a local church, including the following: "Do you promise to support the church in its worship and work to the best of your ability?" In a sense, the question could be restated in these terms: "Do you promise to *love* this particular church?" Invariably, the question is answered in the affirmative; but what is the new member actually promising to do? Is it merely a promise to regard the church in a favorable light and help out if called upon to do so, or is it a promise to be proactive in loving that church? The nature of love argues for the latter. To love the global Church is to love the local church, and to love the local church is to express commitment to her in real, tangible ways.

The title of this chapter, "The Love of the Church," is focused on the love that members are to show *toward* their local church and the Church-at-large. At this point, we need to consider hands-on ways that a member can be a faithful, active part of a local church; in other words, we will consider opportunities for hands-on, tangible expressions of love for your church, God's Church—Christ's Bride.

Needless to say, the following list is *not* exhaustive.[2] However, it helps get our wheels spinning about how we can move from abstract thoughts about loving the Church to more particular ones.

Giving

It has been said that if you want to see what is *really* precious to a person, look at the person's checkbook ledger (you might want to get the person's permission first). Once you have eliminated the essentials—rent or mortgage, food, the usual bills—where does the person's income go? Disposable income is just that; it is income that can be disposed as the owner sees fit. It can be saved, it can be invested, it can be given to charity, it can buy ice cream. It can even do a combination of the above. Whatever the case, decisions about money say a great deal about the priorities of the decision-maker.

What does the Bible say to the believer about giving to the local church?

Interestingly, there is a surprising amount of leeway provided in Scripture. Though giving is an assumed part of the Christian life (Jesus says in the Sermon on the Mount *"when* you give," not *"if* you give"), the *character* of this giving is of utmost importance.

In Paul's second biblical letter to the church in Corinth, he could make this very freeing assertion: "Each man should give what he has decided in his heart to give, not reluctantly or under compulsion, for God loves a cheerful giver" (2 Cor. 9:7). Earlier, however, in the same letter, he reminds them (and us) of a piercing reality: "For you know the grace of our Lord Jesus Christ, that though he was rich, yet for your sakes he became poor, so that you through his poverty might become rich" (8:9).

These two truths serve as guardrails in our thinking about monetary contributions to the local church. On the one hand, there is no divine gun being held to our head, demanding that the ten dollar bill we were going to put in the offering plate be replaced with a hundred dollar bill, or *else*. On the other hand, we should remember that our standard for what true giving looks like is a Savior who was willing to give up the infinite riches and wealth of heaven for the poverty of becoming a sin-bearing Servant, that His people might become eternally blessed beyond measure.

The latter point seems particularly important, since local churches often confine their regular teaching on giving (sometimes referred to as the annual "stewardship season") to biblical passages dealing with the tithe, i.e., the giving of ten percent of one's gross income. Such passages must be dealt with as part of the whole of Scripture. To limit, however, one's understanding of financial participation in the local church to the tithe seems wrongheaded.

Just think about it. If believers who lived on the *other* side of the cross—believers who knew the rigorous demands of regular animal sacrifices and Old Testament dietary restrictions—were required to give ten percent of their gross income as an expression of gratitude for God's faithfulness and forgiveness, *what sort of giving should characterize New Testament believers?*

- We know that the means by which God resolved the very real dilemma of a sin-hating God accepting sinful people is that He sacrificed His one and only Son!
- We now know the reality behind the "copy and shadow" (see Heb. 8:5) of Old Testament public worship. Everything from animal sacrifices to temple furniture was pointing ahead to news that could only be described as "too good to be true," that God the Son would come to earth to live the perfect life that His people would never live, and die the death that they so richly deserved.

We know the full truth, displayed in all its glory.

Should ten percent be the point at which we breathe a financial sigh of relief and say, "Well, I'm glad we got *that* over with"?

Giving money to the local church, particularly as part of the corporate worship of that church (1 Cor. 16:2), is truly one of the privileges of God's people. Though involvement in the work of the kingdom will require that believers give toward civic causes, school endowments, and other charities, giving to the local church is how we tangibly demonstrate that we are beginning to grasp how gracious God has been to us. Grace begets grace, and it shows itself in the offering plate.

Though relevant to every age group, perhaps this matter of giving to the local church should be underscored for college-age believers. Unless they happen to attend college in their hometown, or have transferred their membership to a church near their school, collegiate believers are typically not members of the church they attend. They can feel a certain detachment from the financial obligations of that local church. That fact, coupled with the financial struggles that many students undergo, often leads to a disturbing trend: *probably more hands handle offering plates and do **not** place something inside them in college area churches than any others in the nation.*

To be fair, attending one church while belonging to one elsewhere does present challenges. Do I send my financial gifts back to the church where I am a member, or do I give my gifts to this church while the Lord has me here? Again, the Bible is not cut-and-dry about such questions, but one frequently overlooked Scripture is worth noting: "Anyone who receives instruction in the word must share all good things with his instructor" (Gal. 6:6).

Imagine the negative response of listeners if a preacher harped on this verse! It is from God's Word, nonetheless. Elsewhere, Paul reminds us of a similar truth when he writes that "those who preach the gospel should receive their living from the gospel" (1 Cor. 9:14).

This is particularly relevant to collegiate Christians. College years are often when a person starts looking at life through adult eyes. Biblical truth either comes to light for the first time or takes on greater light. It is appropriate that students begin to learn not only the responsibility, but also the *privilege,* of loving the local church with their gifts.

Confrontation

No one enjoys awkwardness. When we get together for Thanksgiving at a young cook's home, a protracted silence at the dinner table often compels someone to wince: "Well, everything certainly is *delicious.*" If someone on-stage hits a wrong note, everyone silently agonizes. Awkwardness is not fun.

It should be no surprise, then, that we do not relish the thought of sitting down and talking to someone about sin—observable, known breaches of God's commandments (misusing God's name, lying, cheating, adultery, etc.).

Consider an example. If a fellow member of your church allowed you to come over to his house and use his computer, and you stumbled upon downloaded pornographic material, how would you handle it?

- You could gossip about the person, perhaps even to fellow members of the church. This might even provide the added benefit of feeling better about yourself by comparison.
- You could ignore the behavior and pretend that it never really happened, comforting yourself in the knowledge that you were simply trying to practice Christian love (after all, love "keeps no record of wrongs").
- You could even do what often causes the least discomfort of all—simply write him off.

Why would fellow members of a local church ever want to engage in the messy business of confronting one another's sin head-on? It can make the confronter a nervous wreck, terribly wound the recipient, and at least temporarily fracture a friendship. Why do it?

Consider these reasons for loving, biblical confrontation:

1. Confrontation is commanded for God's people.

Christians are *commanded* to confront one another in the face of known sin. In Matthew 18, Jesus gives the following instructions about the steps of what is known as church discipline:

> If your brother sins against you, go and show him his fault, just between the two of you. If he listens to you, you have won your brother over. But if he will not listen, take one or two others along, so that "every matter may be established by the testimony of two or three witnesses." If he refuses to listen to them, tell it to the church; and if he refuses to listen even to the church, treat him as you would a pagan or a tax collector. (vv. 15–17)

Interestingly, Jesus commands that the process of confrontation of sin should begin at a one-to-one level. *Church discipline does not begin with dramatic, public exposures of sin.* Biblical confrontation begins, by divine command, with two professing believers talking privately. Jesus gives a similar command in Luke 17:3: "If your brother sins, rebuke him, and if he repents, forgive him."

The point is all too clear. Confrontation is not a vague ideal; it is commanded for believers in God's Word.

2. Confrontation is motivated by Christian love.

Perhaps one of the most familiar phrases from the Old Testament, and one that is quoted throughout the New, is "love your neighbor as yourself." However, what may not be as familiar is the context in which this phrase appears. It reads: "Do not hate your brother in your heart. *Rebuke your neighbor frankly* so you will not share in his guilt. Do not seek revenge or bear a grudge against one of your people, but *love your neighbor as yourself.* I am the LORD" (Lev. 19:17-18).[3]

Interestingly, this passage provides us with what Christ called the second greatest commandment, but it is wrapped in the context of exercising biblical confrontation. Love, not resentment or anger, motivates biblical confrontation of sin.

Other Scriptures echo this same truth. David wrote, "Let a righteous man strike me—it is a *kindness;* let him rebuke me—it is *oil on my head.* My head will not refuse it" (Ps. 141:5). Proverbs gives us these assertions: "Better is open rebuke than hidden *love.* Wounds from a friend can be trusted, but an enemy multiplies kisses" (27:5-6).[4] The latter even recognizes that wounding sensation that comes with receiving such confrontation. Even given in love, biblical confrontation may *feel* like hurtful attack. But the Scriptures remain clear: such honest feedback is perhaps the ultimate litmus test for discovering who truly loves us, and whom we truly love.

3. Confrontation strives for an individual's restoration.

The goal of all this is needed repentance and restoration. Direct confrontation is never to be a veiled attack. Rather, it is a God-given opportunity for Christians to demonstrate that they really believe that we are as sinful as the Bible says we are, and that we really need each other's help as much as the Bible says we do.

Paul gives us this exhortation: "Brothers, if someone is caught in a sin, you who are spiritual should restore him gently. But watch yourself, or you also may be tempted" (Gal. 6:1). Again, we are reminded of our *mutual frailty*. We must strive to restore wandering brothers and sisters, all the while remembering we are fellow sinners, equally needing the grace of God.

Those who listen to such confrontation will once again find themselves in the company of those who fear God. Proverbs tells us, "He who listens to a life-giving rebuke will be at home among the wise" (Prov. 15:31). This should encourage us to take up this difficult task! Godly rebuke is "life-giving."

It is difficult to overstate the necessity that these truths be put into practice in local churches. Perhaps nothing does more to drive people away from the local church than the proverbial infighting, squabbling, and pettiness that pastors and members alike can exhibit. What is the antidote?

Jesus said, "By this all men will know that you are my disciples, if you love one another" (John 13:35). The "love" of which He spoke is not a vague sort of public niceness, niceness that appears to care but refuses to do anything unsettling. No, this is the sort of love that God has shown us, a tenacious commitment to another that manifests itself by turning light where only darkness was desired. If this occurred more often in churches, it might actually begin to communicate to those watching that we love each other as much as we claim.

Hospitality

In the course of a normal day (if there is such a thing), we wake up, conduct our morning ritual, go to work, maybe run errands afterwards, and then go home. In the midst of our workday, there will be unexpected calls, interruptions, and perhaps even emergencies. If there is anything we do *not* want upon our return home, it is additional intrusion. When it comes to our weekends, that feeling can grow even stronger. "I've worked hard all week. This is 'Me Time.'" Needless to say, this mindset is not one that rejoices at the thought of inviting others into our home, feeding them (at *our* expense), and engaging them in conversation. Hospitality is already waging an uphill battle.

The exercise of hospitality may feel like an optional aspect of the Christian life, but it is worth stopping and considering its emphasis in the Scriptures.

- Abraham extended it to strangers (who ended up being the Lord and two angels). (Gen. 18:1ff.)
- Jesus speaks of extending it not only to "your friends,

your brothers or relatives, or your rich neighbors," but also to "the poor, the crippled, the lame, the blind" (Luke 14:12–13).

+ Paul *commands* the church in Rome to practice it (Rom. 12:13).

+ In *both* lists of credentials for elders in the church, being hospitable is assigned the status of a "must" (1 Tim. 3:2; Titus 1:8).

+ Peter *commands* the practice of it as well, and stipulates that it should be done "without grumbling" (1 Pet. 4:9).

Why is hospitality assigned such importance in the Bible? We get a clue by considering a recurring motif in Jesus' life. Luke records that when Jesus went to the house of Levi the tax collector (a hated occupation), He was asked by the religious leaders of His day, "Why do you eat and drink with tax collectors and 'sinners'?" (Luke 5:30). Later, it is recorded that these same religious leaders laid this charge at Jesus' door: "This man welcomes sinners and eats with them" (15:2).

Although these episodes do not describe Jesus providing food or lodging for guests, they demonstrate a key principle for understanding hospitality: *To be under the same roof with someone and to eat with that person is to identify with that person intimately.*

When we invite our brothers and sisters in the local church (and others, as well) into our homes, we tangibly demonstrate that we believe ourselves to be on a level playing field.

But along with coming to grips with hospitality's place in Scripture, we must come to grips with why we tend to neglect it as part of the Christian life. What sorts of barriers are we encountering in our own hearts and minds as we think about welcoming others into our homes?

"My home is a wreck."

This pressure may be more from within than from without. Many of us seem to fear that if someone comes into our home to eat or to stay overnight, and if every room in our home does not look photoworthy for *Better Homes and Gardens,* then our guest(s) will be appalled, storm out the door, and begin a massive smear campaign about our slovenly ways.

This usually does not happen.

Yes, we should strive for some semblance of order in our lives and homes, and yes, there is a sense in which we communicate our respect for our guests by cleaning up for them. Yet, practically anyone you will ever have into your home understands that real living in a real home is not conducive to twenty-four-hour tidiness. Furthermore, practically anyone you will ever invite into your home not only appreciates the offering of a meal or lodging, but is probably pleasantly surprised. If and when they do come under your roof, it is highly unlikely that they will post photos of what they find there on the Internet. (Disclaimer: the above statement is not a guarantee!)

"I simply don't have the time."

This may be the most common objection to practicing hospitality.

Time is our most precious commodity, and we all feel that we do not have enough of it. By the same token, as we make decisions daily about what we will and will not do, we form priorities in our minds. There are those things which we *must* do: eat, sleep, earn income, pay bills. Then there are those things which we *may* do: exercise, read, cultivate true friendships, and pursue outside interests.

In regard to the latter group, we typically say, "I just don't have time to . . ." Usually what we mean is that there is no obvious block of time that will make these activities convenient and easy.

However, many a heart patient has found late in life that what was thought to be a "may" (in this case, exercise) is actually more of a "must." Human bodies that are not properly managed through proper diet and exercise almost always deteriorate faster. Intellectually, such patients knew that to be a reasonable assertion. A medical crisis, though, forced the issue.

The Scriptures cry out to us: "You need to have others, especially fellow believers, in your home." However, we may still have this activity under the "may" category in our minds. Scripture calls us to move hospitality into the "must" category. If there does not seem to be time to do it, then we must make time to do it.

"I can't afford it."

This might be a reasonable objection, if hospitality always involved seven-course meals. But, again, this objection probably arises more from internal pressures than external ones. If we have a home, then we already have a location ("home base") in which to practice hospitality. If someone stays overnight, we will end up washing sheets and bath towels, which we would have eventually done anyway. Aside from that, we can provide a meal or meals for our guests (again, not five-star enterprises). It can be store-bought lasagna. It can be hamburgers.

Practicing hospitality is a heart issue. These sorts of mental and emotional barriers are typically symptomatic of a more profound problem of the heart, namely, that we do not wish to be bothered with the concerns of others—even our brothers and sisters in the church. Philosopher and theologian Francis Schaeffer spoke of Christians being seduced by the god of personal peace and affluence, and the accuracy of his words is evident in our general hesitancy to open our homes to others.

Perhaps it would help our motivation if we saw something of the beauty in what can be accomplished through hospitality in the local church. For instance, a *persistent* frustration for college students who become involved with a local church is that they often feel that few people in the church really know them, and vice versa. One young lady expressed it this way: "I feel like I'm outside a house, looking in through the window at the family, wishing I could be a part of it." Typically, such students point to the absence of invitations into homes, as well as not being known by name, as indications of why they feel frustrated.

Obviously, it is impossible for each church member single-handedly to remedy such frustrations. But think how different the landscape might look if members of college-area churches began to identify two or three students who participated in the worship of that church, particularly if the students had themselves become members. It need not be a church program, complete with sign-up posters and fliers in the Sunday bulletin. It could simply be an act of Christian love that members take up as they come to grips with the wonderful opportunity God has placed in their own backyard.

But where would they begin? This could be addressed by yet another opportunity for hospitality. Some churches, in order to aid the elders in shepherding the members, divide the members and even regular visitors into smaller groups. For instance, a church of two hundred members may have eight elders; if each elder had a group of twenty-five for whom he was responsible, this would help not only him, but the twenty-five as well. He would know which ones of the two hundred members upon whom he should focus particular attention, and they would know which elder they should call first for prayer, information, counsel, etc.

What a golden opportunity this could be for what we might call "focused hospitality." The members within each group could begin to develop the more regular exercise of hospitality with other members of that same group. Hospitality within the local church needs to begin somewhere; in such groups, it could begin with each other. Some churches even have weekly meetings in homes of such groups, sometimes being led by the elder assigned to that group. This could be yet another avenue for members of college-area churches to have more outreach. The students who participated in these small groups would not so easily blend with other unknown visitors. The small-group participants would know their names, and they would be an obvious starting place for hospitality to college students. As for the students themselves, it is difficult to measure the value that they would place upon the regular opportunity to be in an adult's home.

These are possible scenarios, but they are not far-fetched ones. What should be obvious is that hospitality holds great potential for mutual Christian joy. However, there may be an even greater benefit. If the church is in dire need of communicating to her people that the church is the *people*, not a *building*, hospitality is a tremendous means of conveying that reality.

Prayer

On this subject we do not lack for biblical material and "proof texts." The only problem is that the biblical material is overwhelming! At practically every turn, we are confronted with the priority that prayer is to hold in the Christian's life. Certainly, then, we must agree that praying for the local church is a means of manifesting true love for her.

Also, there is so much for which to pray. Perhaps you have been involved in a church that had some sort of weekly prayer meeting, and that provided a list of prayer requests for those who attended. If so, you may know the experience of looking at a rather daunting list and feeling tired before you even began. Family concerns, issues at work, national and international concerns, illnesses, surgeries, outreach to others, upcoming events. So much to pray, so little time— and energy.

So, for what *should* we pray when we pray for the local church? Obviously, each congregation of believers will present unique opportunities for prayer, but is there some sort of *meta*concern—that is, an over-arching concern—that should find a regular place in the prayers of church members?

Actually, there is; it is something called *revival.*

In American church lingo, *revival* typically means when a church conducts a special meeting, or series of meetings, with a particularly evangelistic focus, and probably with special speakers and music. However, this is not the historic understanding of what Christians for centuries have meant by *revival.* Rather, revival has been understood as a supernatural work of the Holy Spirit, one that cannot be scheduled (unlike the definition above).

In such a work of the Spirit, multitudes of non-Christians are brought under conviction of sin and experience an accompanying awe at the holiness of God, and then come in droves to Christ for salvation. Furthermore, during such times, those who were already Christians seem to have newfound delight in the glory of God and the wonder of the gospel, and the effects of it can be felt everywhere from their Sunday worship to their home life, their work ethic to their outreach.

One 19th-century hymn has this refrain: "Showers of blessing, showers of blessing we need; mercy-drops round us are falling, but for the showers we plead." We could say that the "mercy-drops" are the normal, ongoing work of the Holy Spirit, but the "showers" are times of revival.

It would be inappropriate to put all of our church-related eggs into the basket of revival, as if to say that everything in a local church is "on hold" until God sends such a downpour of blessing. We would be hard-pressed, however, to think of a more urgent concern in our prayer for the local church.

Do we want to see God's name "hallowed"?

Do we want the members of the local church to drink more deeply of the goodness of the gospel of Jesus Christ?

Do we want to see preaching, the sacraments, and pastoring taken up by church leaders with newfound energy?

Do we want to see churches full, and see their outreach increase?

If we do, then we want revival.

However, we should also note that there is an unmistakable pattern in the history of revivals. Though true revival cannot be produced by any measures on our part, all true revivals have been preceded by times of intense prayer. Perhaps this sounds like something of a paradox, but the fact remains: Christians cannot force God's hand to send revivals, but such times are always preceded by believers crying out to God. This is convicting, because we delight at the thought of God supernaturally accomplishing such profound change in our churches, but we are sluggish in the necessary work of pleading for Him to do so. One Christian expressed the problem this way:

> We long for revivals; we speak of revivals, we
> work for revivals; and we even pray a little for them.
> But we do not enter upon that labor in prayer,

which is the essential preparation for every revival. . . .

The work of the Spirit can be compared to mining. The Spirit's work is to blast to pieces the sinner's hardness of heart and his frivolous opposition to God. The period of the awakening can be likened to the time when the blasts are fired. The time between the awakenings corresponds, on the other hand, to the time when the deep holes are being bored with great effort into the hard rock.

To bore these holes is hard and difficult and a task which tries one's patience. To light the fuse and fire the shot is not only easy but also very interesting work. One sees "results" from such work. It creates interest, too; shots resound, and pieces fly in every direction!

It takes trained workmen to do the boring. Anybody can light a fuse.[5]

If we love the local church, we must see ourselves as the "workmen" willing to take up the gritty labor of pleading with God to revive us. The temptation is to abdicate this prayer responsibility to someone else and wait in the wings for the exciting times to begin. To love a church, though, is to be willing to plead on her behalf.[6]

Planning

To love someone necessitates including that person in your plans.

Husbands are notorious for failing to tell their wives that a couple of friends are coming for supper . . . in thirty minutes! ("That's not a problem, is it?") Teenage children have been known to inform parents that they must purchase materials for a science fair project—which is due in twelve hours. The frustration that accompanies these scenarios stems from the fact that we instinctively expect to be a part of the plans of those we love. In a sense, this is an outworking of the fact that love is kind and is *not* rude (1 Cor. 13:4, 5).

This principle holds true in our love for a church as well. Is she included in our thinking and planning? Consider just two examples.

A college senior who is a Christian assembles his winning résumé, completes a round of interviews, and is given three offers. After much reflection, prayer, and advice from others, he decides to accept a position that has some exciting opportunities, but it is located in an unfamiliar part of the country. Upon graduation, he says his good-byes, loads the moving van, and sets up shop in his new surroundings. His first few days there go well, but as the weekend approaches, a question moves from the back of his mind to the forefront: "I wonder where I will go to church?"

This question should have been asked earlier! If the local church is indeed God's unique institution for His people's growth and witness, this should have been an integral part of the decision-making process. For whatever length of time he remains in this particular area, he will be directly affected by the church he joins. This will be where he hears the Word of God, where he participates in the sacraments, and where he is pastored. This is quite a different consideration from those of the local restaurant scene or movie rental options.

Consider another example in the lives of believers. As two young parents plan their week, they wrestle with the barrage of their children's activities. The options of "enriching" activities for their children is endless, and they want the best for their children. This family's choices have ended up including music lessons and involvement on several sports teams. As the obligations of these activities begin to pile up and even overlap, the parents are confronted with prioritizing what their children will do and will *not* do.

What priority will these parents assign to their children's involvement in the local church? When Luke describes the lifestyle of the three thousand Christians converted at Pentecost, he writes that they *"devoted* themselves to the apostles' teaching and to the fellowship, to the breaking of bread and to prayer" (Acts 2:42). When the apostle Peter addressed this same group earlier, he described the gospel as being "for you *and your children* and for all who are far off—for all whom the Lord our God will call" (v. 39).[7] In other words, the picture that is provided of the activities of the Jerusalem church is not a picture of adults assembling without children. The *families* devoted themselves to what the church was doing.

This is significant, because believing parents often are willing to forfeit their children's participation in the local church for yet another "enriching" commitment. Sadly, Sundays even are allowed to become yet another day of rushing to activities that do not include the local church.

Are such activities inherently wrong? Of course not. One of the most freeing aspects of the Christian life is the biblical insistence that "whether you eat or drink or whatever you do, do it all for the glory of God" (1 Cor. 10:31). However, if a child becomes a teenager and has excelled at a sport and a musical instrument but has little or no idea what the Lord's Supper means or how the fourth commandment is a blessing, can we really say that this child has been, biblically speaking, enriched?

Love Your Local Church

Surely you have seen the bumper sticker by now. It simply reads, "Think Globally, Act Locally." The point is well made. All of us should concern ourselves with the challenges that face all people everywhere, but that concern cannot be expressed everywhere. We demonstrate our concern by acting and living where we are.

Jesus Christ loves the Church. He loves her so much that He died for her. As His people are conformed to His likeness (Rom. 8:29), they love what He loves. Hence, they love the Church, His bride. But where does that love for the Church, a global entity, find its expression?

It finds expression in loving the local church.

What is the best reason for going to a church's prayer meeting when you feel too tired to pray? What is the best reason for allowing other Christians into your home when all you want is to be left alone?

The answer is simple. It is the same reason you go out of your way for your spouse or children or siblings or parents: love.

The best reason is that if Christ loved the Church enough to die for her, if He passionately loves her still, and if believers are being changed into His likeness, then we can love the local church. Think globally, love locally.

8

The Future of the Church

Mid toil and tribulation, and tumult of her war,
she waits the consummation of peace for evermore;
till with the vision glorious her longing eyes are blessed,
and the great Church victorious shall be the Church at rest.

~ Samuel John Stone

A golf instructor often will work with his student on his follow through, his "finishing swing." Mistakes in take-back, down-swing, and contact point can sometimes be corrected by thinking through where the golf club will finish, known as the follow-through. Likewise, a correct view of the future of the Church (where it is headed and how it will get there) can correct much that is misguided in its present form of ministry.

Therefore, in this chapter, we will consider what we can do in the "here and now" to be faithful Church people. We will also consider the destiny of the Lord's Body, the "then and there." The hope is that a clear view of the future will direct our present practice.

Here and Now

Much of the material in this book was presented recently at a

conference for youth ministers. One particularly cynical youth pastor approached me after the seminar and began his comments this
way, "All I have to say is, yeah . . . maybe in perfect world." His point
was that the ideal of a local church operating on a truly biblical
model is too much to hope for in this life and therefore impractical
for most to adopt.

Yet the Lord Jesus loved the Church enough to die for her, so I can
love her enough to be patient with her and commit myself to doing
and being all that I can in order to see her to where God is taking her.
Any consideration of the principles contained in this book must
include a consideration of the "What now . . . ?" To be a faithful
member of the Lord's Church, what are the concrete responsibilities
that rest upon the believer in the light of these insights?

Change your expectations

With pastoral ministry having degenerated into the world of the
"wannabe" CEO, it is safe to sit in the pews next Sunday and assume
certain things about your pastor.

First, you can assume that your pastor is spending most of his time
not doing half of the things he was trained to do in good seminaries
these days. During his training, your pastor was energized by the
study of the Word of God, its application to the lives of those for
whom he daily prayed, and a vision of one-to-one ministry that
included heart-felt evangelism and life-deepening discipleship. A
quick look at his weekly schedule will clearly show just how little of
this activity fills up his week.

Second, and in many ways this is a consequence of the first, you can almost assume that your pastor is suffering from (or fast on his way to) burnout. Vague job descriptions, insecurities about the "success" of his ministry, as well as personal life struggles in the fishbowl of congregational expectations are enough to drive even the most idealistic of pastors into thoughts of leaving the ministry or into daydreaming of the "greener pastures" of other congregations.

Therefore, each member of a congregation must begin to change his expectations of what the pastor is called by God to do. By drawing from the lessons learned in the chapter, "The Business of the Church," we must encourage our pastors self-consciously to reclaim their true vocation: giving themselves to the study of the Word, the joy of administering the Sacraments, and praying for, and ministering to, their flock.

Not only that, but they must willfully withdraw themselves from such tasks not clearly in their realm of their responsibilities. Taking his cue from the Apostles in Acts 6, the minister must determine that to be too busy to study the Word and pray for his people is to have abdicated his first responsibility to his congregation and call.

This is more than just encouraging your pastor to do a better job at delegating. It is a call for believers to reconsider what "church" is and does. How much of what a pastor does in the space of his workweek has little or nothing to do with the biblically defined responsibilities of a local expression of the body of Christ? Someone might object to this by saying, "But my pastor says that he doesn't mind the administrative tasks. He feels like Saturday afternoon is plenty of time for him to prepare his sermons and teach the congregation." To this, we can only say that it very well might be the case that your pastor might need to question whether or not he is indeed called to be a minister.

If I find myself without the gifts, the inward desire, and the outward confirmation of the Church to preach and to pray for my people, it may very well be that my calling lies somewhere else in the Kingdom of God. There is nothing less spiritual about taking a job in the "secular" world and abandoning the work in the institutional Church, especially when my gifts and abilities reveal that I do not belong there. One of the more difficult responsibilities in which a group of elders might find themselves is to have to encourage their pastor to find work elsewhere in God's Kingdom. It might also be the kindest thing they have ever done for him.

Build relationships

The most fundamental definition of the Church is the covenantal bond that you have with the person sitting next to you in the pew. Therefore, at the heart of your responsibilities in the Church must be *intentionality* in building relationships with others in your congregation. This is more than just starting a supper club with a few of those congregation members with whom you have the most in common. This means bringing even those with whom you would not naturally be inclined to relate into the fellowship of your home, your time, and your life.

The *Westminster Confession of Faith*, in its chapter entitled "The

Communion of the Saints," succinctly puts it:

> Saints by profession are bound to maintain an holy fellowship and communion in the worship of God, and in performing such other spiritual services as tend to their mutual edification; as also in relieving each other in outward things, according to their several abilities and necessities. Which communion, as God offereth opportunity, is to be extended unto all those who, in every place, call upon the name of the Lord Jesus.[1]

The first inventory that a believer ought to take in consideration of his responsibilities to the local body is of the "spiritual services as tend to [the] mutual edification" of the people in the congregation. In other words, where is my responsibility to this body spiritually and how am I fulfilling that responsibility? Do I have gifts of teaching? If so, then am I teaching? Do I have gifts of service? If so, then whom in the congregation in the last month have I served without expectation of return? How often this week have I prayed for the members in my congregation in need and the pastors and elders who oversee them?

Secondly, you as a believer ought to take an inventory of your ability to "[relieve] each other in outward things." How many times this month has my family cut a check *not* to the church (so that I can write it off on my taxes this year) but to the man who just lost his job and can not pay his bills this month? How faithful have I been to give sacrificially of my possessions to those in need?

Finally, every believer ought to take stock of the people to whom he has offered himself. Have I been guilty of serving only those whom I like, or those with whom I have something in common? Have I reached out only to the "pretty people" of my congregation? Or have I realized that it is to the "least of the brethren" that Jesus identified Himself? The Confession here warns us that our service "is to be extended unto all those who, in every place, call upon the name of the Lord Jesus."

C.S. Lewis writes in his wonderful sermon "The Weight of Glory":

> It is in the light of these possibilities, it is with the awe and the circumspection proper to them, that we should conduct all our dealings with one another, all friendships, all loves, all play, all politics. There are no *ordinary* people. You have never talked to a mere mortal. . . . But it is immortals whom we joke with, work with, marry, snub and exploit—immortal horrors or everlasting splendours.[2]

Take responsibility in the Kingdom of God

The question could reasonably be asked concerning the world at large, "Well, if the Church *as an institution* is to withdraw into Her sphere and commit Herself to those responsibilities that are distinctive to that sphere, who is responsible for carrying the Kingdom of

God into the world?" The answer is . . . the *members* of the Church, or, in other words, *you*!

Even to ask the question about who is going to reach the world with the new value system of the Kingdom of God is to prove that you have been lulled to sleep by an abdication of your responsibilities.

Every believer is to serve the poor. *Every* believer is to give of his possessions to help the needy. *Every* believer is to clothe those who are naked. *Every* believer is to witness to his co-workers. *Every* believer is to visit those who are in prison. *Every* believer is to house those who are homeless. These responsibilities do not fall in the lap of some committee of your church. They fall in the lap of every believer who names the name of Jesus Christ as Lord.

To sit in the pews week after week with arms folded saying, *"Tsk, tsk,* someone ought to do something about that," is to admit that you have seen a need in the Kingdom of God and refused to meet it. Christ's condemnation for those who have refused to take responsibility for social ills that they have clearly seen is unequivocal:

> "They also will answer, 'Lord, when did we see you hungry or thirsty or a stranger or needing clothes or sick or in prison, and did not help you?'
>
> "He will reply, 'I tell you the truth, whatever you did not do for one of the least of these, you did not do for me.'
>
> "Then they will go away to eternal punishment, but the righteous to eternal life." [3]

When was the last time you gathered a group of like-minded individuals in your community for the purpose of resolving yourselves to do something about some injustice, some poverty, some lack that was present before your very eyes? Ministry in deed as well as in word is vitally necessary if the Kingdom of God is to be spread abroad, and the responsibility can be taken tomorrow if you, as a believer, are willing.

The application of this admonition would be incomplete if it were assumed that somehow this didn't apply to pastors as well. It is far too easy for a minister to assume that his vocational responsibilities as a pastor somehow fulfill his obligation to serve those around him. Pastors, when was the last time you took up some personal project in your community that had absolutely nothing to do with your responsibilities at the church? Your family needs to see ministry extended from your own hand in order to demonstrate that your faith is more than just a job.

There and Then

Almost every Sunday, believers from around the world pray what has become known as The Lord's Prayer. Granted, it is decidedly a silly "splitting of hairs," but the title of the "Lord's Prayer" is a misnomer of sorts because the prayer often associated with the it is decidedly *not* the Lord Jesus' prayer. *His* prayer is located in John 17 where we get an amazing glimpse into Jesus' heart and relationship with His Heavenly Father. The prayer in Matthew 6:9-13, however, is the *believer's* prayer. Regardless, every Sunday we rather casually pray through what are some of the most gut wrenching petitions anyone could offer.

For instance, are we really prepared to face the answer to the prayer, "Forgive us our debts, as we forgive our debtors"? This part of the prayer asks God to render forgiveness to His people like unto, or similar to, the forgiveness that believers have extended to those around them. The prayer basically asks this, "Lord, please forgive me in the same manner, and with the same heart, and with the same frequency, that I have forgiven all those around me." How many have heaped judgment upon their heads week after week after praying this prayer, for Jesus' teaching seems to suggest that the great terror of the last day will simply be the answering of that very prayer? He will forgive us as we have forgiven each other.

But notice another petition in the prayer: "Thy will be done on earth as it is in heaven." Do we realize the commitment we make when we pray this? The prayerful heart here begs that God would cause the activity of earth to look like the activity of heaven. The Christian who prays this prayer is committing himself to making this world reflect the business of heaven. Martyn Lloyd-Jones, in his *Commentary on The Sermon on the Mount,* says:

> In heaven the will of God is always being done perfectly. We have only some dim and faint figures of it in the Scriptures, but we have sufficient to know that what is characteristic of heaven is that everyone and everything is waiting upon God

and anxious to glorify and magnify His name. . . .
The supreme desire of all in heaven is to do the
will of God, and thereby to praise and worship
Him. And it should be the desire of every true
Christian, says our Lord here, that all on earth
should be the same.[4]

The point is this: everything in which a Christian engages in this
life is to prepare him for heaven. Every activity, every ambition, every
endeavor, every goal ought to be aimed at making a soul meet for
glory. The reverse is also true. Anything in which I am engaged that
is not preparing me for heaven is a waste. To pray this petition is
immediately to prioritize all of life as well as set an agenda for the
pilgrimage of the Church while it still sojourns on earth.

The doctrines of justification and sanctification have always been
at the heart of any right understanding of a biblical view of salvation.
Justification is the doctrine that God declares sinners to be righteous
on the basis of the merit of the Mediator, Jesus Christ. It is received
by faith alone. Sanctification is the doctrine that the declaration
made by God will always produce holiness in the life. Sin will be put
to death and righteousness will be brought to life. Justification represents the entrance into the Christian life while sanctification
describes its continuation.

But isn't the doctrine of salvation truncated without a view
towards the *goal* of the Christian life?

Without a view toward the *ends* of salvation, hasn't the Church failed to equip her membership for life in the Kingdom of God? There can be little doubt that the doctrine of glorification needs fresh attention in our day.

Glorification is the doctrine that God will one day raise His elect with resurrection bodies (like that of the resurrection body of the Lord Jesus) to join him in eternal fellowship with Him. At that time the Church will join those around the throne of God who "never stop saying: 'Holy, holy, holy is the Lord God Almighty, who was, and is, and is to come.'"[5]

In chapter 19 of Revelation, the Church gathers as the Bride of Christ coming to the wedding feast prepared for her by the Lamb. Verse 8 says, "Fine linen, bright and clean, was given to her to wear." Expounding his meaning, John says, "Fine linen stands for the righteous acts of the saints." Therefore, the activity of the Church in glory will consist primarily in the praise of God combined with perfect obedience to the will of God.

So the "Lord's Prayer" is a vivid statement of commitment that whatever is done in the Church today will ultimately lend itself to preparing the people of God for holiness and eternal praise. The doctrine of glorification instructs the Church in her present practice to put away activity that does not contribute to igniting her heart in praise and pushing her forward to living obedience to the will of God.

Therefore, the Church ought to have the flavor of heaven. This, by the way, is part of the rationale behind believers dressing up when they gather in their "Sunday best." Believers have at times dressed up in order to attend worship for the simple fact that they are indeed playing "dress up." When the Church gathers as the corporate body of believers, they gather, among other things, to anticipate the glory that awaits them. Therefore, they wear their best clothes in anticipation of the "fine linen" which they will wear on that great day before the throne.[6]

Therefore, if our churches are to mirror heaven, it is only right that they be vividly aware of what their responsibilities in heaven will be. Theologians have traditionally spoken of the Church Militant and the Church Triumphant. While on earth, the Church works and wars against the flesh and the Devil. But, when finally home, the Church will take on the responsibility for which she was created.

Donald MacLeod, Scottish theologian at Edinburgh, describes three primary activities in which the Church will be engaged in eternity.

First among them is *work*. Despite many unhealthy (and indeed, unbiblical) attitudes towards labor, God created and instituted work at the beginning of His creation in the Creation Mandate. In Genesis 1:28, God instructs His creatures to "fill the earth and subdue it." This command was issued before the Fall. Frustration in work is a result of the Fall, but work itself is a mandate of God for all mankind in whatever spiritual state.

This should not surprise us that we will have responsibility in heaven. Our resurrection bodies will, by definition, be physical. Therefore, it is natural to expect that our labor will be physical. It is a Gnostic error (which elevates the spiritual over the physical) that envisions heaven as a collection of disembodied souls. Macleod comments:

Paradise was no mere seminary where Adam and

Eve whiled away the hours in theological discussion. I'm sure they did that, and that they did it with more relish than any of my students. But Eden offered scope for art, science and technology as well as theology. The same will doubtless be true of the world to come. Bearing the image of the heavenly, we shall explore, colonise, serve, keep and enhance our magnificent environment . . . The scenario is a thrilling one: brilliant minds in powerful bodies in a transformed universe. With energy, dexterity, and athleticism here undreamed of, we shall explore horizons beyond our wildest imaginings.[7]

One evening while watching the Discovery Channel on cable television, a young man listened to an astrophysicist expound his theories of the origins of the universe. After a brief discussion on the massive size of the universe and its seemingly unending bounds, the commentator said something like, "So when I look at the size of the universe, I am simply unwilling to believe that there was some creative design behind it. I mean, it can't all be just *for us* . . . What a waste!"

The scientist was actually very close to the mark. It is mind-blowing to imagine the untold resources that God has implanted in the limitless universe. As believers, we anticipate the never-ending activity of mining that universe for all of its untold treasures and potentialities. The physicist's problem was that he was not acquainted with our lavishing God!

Second, the Church will be engaged in *worship*. Revelation 7:15 says that we will serve Him night and day in His temple. But John says very specifically that in the New Jerusalem there will be no physical temple. He means, then, that all will be the temple. There will be no place in heaven where the very presence of God will not dwell in all of His power and glory.

As a ten-year-old child, I vividly remember asking my father what we would *do* in heaven. As a committed believer, my father rightly answered, "Well son, we will spend eternity praising God." My brow furrowed as I stared at him in silence for a few moments before asking him, "Anything else?" My reaction to the thought of spending an eternity praising God mirrors our culture's reaction to the same notion. Gary Larson, cartoon artist of *The Far Side* cartoon, once pictured a man sitting on a cloud staring into space, apparently having just arrived in heaven and recently acquiring his wings. The thought bubble above his head read, "I wish I'd brought a magazine."

Of course, the reason why the thought of an eternity spent praising God seemed less than an exciting proposition to me was because I was not a Christian. Only the Holy Spirit working through the agency of the Word can enlighten a mind so that it yearns for fellowship with God more than it longs for anything else. However, the question is well worth asking: Does the Church long to be with her God? Is it the preoccupation of the members of the Church to depart and be with the Lord? If not, why not?

The simple answer may very well be that we do not long for heaven because we are quite content here on earth. The affluence of our age will undoubtedly carry with it a high spiritual price. American Christianity has enjoyed a wealth that can only be called opulence by 95 percent of the world's population. Jesus' words, though not a condemnation of wealth *per se,* fail to haunt the souls of Western Christianity as they ought: "How hard it is for a rich man to enter the kingdom of God!" "Hard" because wealth makes the heart content in something other than the riches of Christ in the Gospel.

For years, my failure to be encouraged at the thought of an eternity in heaven was a source of great spiritual discomfort. Why is it so difficult for the heart to grasp these things? Paul addresses the progress of a person's journey toward heaven in 1 Corinthians 13:10ff. "Now we see but a poor reflection as in a mirror; then we shall see face to face. Now I know in part; then I shall know fully, even as I am fully known." (vs. 12) When "perfection" comes, that is, when the Church shall reach her consummation, then our knowledge of God and of ourselves will be "complete." This is not to say that our knowledge in heaven will somehow be exhaustive as the knowledge of God is total.

The passage suggests that our knowledge will change in the *qualitative* sense. Indeed, we shall know "even as we are fully known." That is to say, our knowledge of ourselves will be as clear as the knowledge that God has of us.

This great promise stands as both horrifying and encouraging to the believer's mind. On the one hand, when our knowledge is made "perfect," we shall see our sin from the Father's eyes. We shall feel the treason of what we have called peccadilloes, we shall see how moldy and diseased was our deepest devotion, we shall smell the stench of filth from our best and most righteous deeds. To see the face of God will be at once to grasp the true nature of sin and feel the weight of our rebellion.

However, at the very same moment, "in a flash, in the twinkling of an eye" (1 Cor. 15:52), the heart of every saint will be flooded with the full measure of the love of God in Christ. God the Father will grant every saint the ability to see with white-hot intensity just how much He has longed for them to dwell with them, for them to taste His goodness, for them to behold His glory. Recall to yourself the moment of your greatest spiritual joy, when you, perhaps for the first time, grasped even with the weakest and wavering faith the mercy of God in Christ. Those moments will be multiplied a thousand times over when the Church looks upon her Savior unveiled. Samuel Rutherford understood something of this when he wrote:

> O Christ! He is the fountain, the deep sweet well of love!
> The streams on earth I've tasted, more deep I'll drink above!
> There to an ocean fullness, His mercy doth expand,
> And glory, glory dwelleth, in Emmanuel's land.

To see God "face to face" will be to see the yawning chasm of the offense of our sin open beneath us while at the same time seeing the infinite mountain of God's love filling up that chasm and setting us upon its sure foundation. *Then,* eternity will be too short to utter all His praise.

Macleod says:

> The vision before us (the majesty of God unveiled in the transfigured humanity of Christ) will forbid silence. It will invoke, irresistibly, wonder, love, and praise; and these will find expression not only in the voices of individuals, but in the symphony of all the redeemed. . . . It will be a great harmony, a symphony of grace, awe-inspiring in volume and yet euphonious and melodious as the harp: the response of humanity to the wonderful works of God.[8]

Finally, the Church will experience *rest*. With the lifting of the full effects of the curse upon the Church, there will arise from her a great sigh of comfort and relief; relief from her toils and her persecution; relief from her disappointment and fears; relief from her inner struggles and sleepless nights. There will be eternal relief from every inch of her existence where the curse has taken root.

There, in heaven, the Church will experience the fullness of what her Sabbath was created to foreshadow. The fourth commandment to "Remember the Sabbath day by keeping it holy" has within it an eschatological element. God's command that we set aside a day for worship and rest points forward to the great eternal rest that all God's people will know. The Sabbath day is its own incentive. On that day, all of God's elect will collapse with fatigue, having run the good race and having fought the good fight, into the arms of Jesus, never again to leave. Once more from Macleod:

> Heaven means sharing in the blessedness of God so that in the very depths of our being there is divine contentment, joy and fulfillment. There is total shalom: a sense of sheer well-being. Every need is met. Every longing is fulfilled. Every goal is achieved. Every sense is satisfied. We see him. We are with him. He holds us and hugs us and whispers, *'This is for ever.'*[9]

The Enduring Community

In 1997, the BBC referred to J.R.R. Tolkien's *The Lord of Rings* trilogy as the greatest work of literature of the twentieth century. In it, the tales and adventures of stout little creatures called "hobbits" are recounted. Frodo and his faithful companion Sam manage to survive epic adventures in their battle with the forces of evil. Yet, once survived and returned, Frodo finds that he cannot really come home. Having tasted the adventure and been pierced with the wound of the weight of what he has experienced, he longs to cross the Great Sea into the West. There is where the Elves long to be and know true rest for themselves.

> One evening Sam came into the study and found his master looking very strange. He was very

pale and his eyes seemed to see things far away.

"What's the matter, Mr. Frodo?" said Sam. "I am wounded," he answered. "Wounded; it will never really heal."[10]

For those of us still left, life in the Church Militant is a wound. We have been wounded by our own foolishness and passions. Yet we have also felt the wound of the love of God, piercing us deeper than we knew any could, and showing us a vision of true fellowship with Him, in a day when all will be set right and holiness will come naturally, our own "Western Lands."

Until that time, we pray, we search the Scriptures, we give spiritual counsel, we do what the Church has always done.

In the beginning, God gathered a Church. Throughout the Old Testament, He matured her and chastened her. He atoned for her sin through His Son, Jesus Christ. He "bar mitzvah-ed" her at Pentecost by giving her His Holy Spirit. His angels now roam throughout the four corners of the Earth, gathering His elect, His Church. One day, He will present her as a spotless Bride to His Son, where they will commune for eternity. God has always been about the business of His Church. It is our heritage, our home, and our hope. It is the Enduring Community.

Notes

1 The Disappointment of the Church

1. Cited in William D. Hendricks' *Exit Interviews* (Chicago: Moody, 1993), 252.

2. Iain H. Murray, *David Martyn Lloyd-Jones: The First Forty Years 1899-1939* (Carlisle, PA: Banner of Truth Trust, 1982), 138.

2 The Idea of the Church

1. Michael Scott Horton, *Putting Amazing Back into Grace* (Nashville: Thomas Nelson Publishers, 1991), xi. Wayne Mack and David Swavely's book *Life in the Father's House: A Member's Guide to the Local Church* has this to say about this important point, ". . . the church . . . actually holds up the truth. Or to put it in more graphic (and perhaps shocking) terms, God's truth is not able to stand without the church. . . . The implication of Paul's words is that the truth would fall into disaster if the church did not exist." Mack and Swavely, *House* (Phillipsburg, NJ: P&R, 1996), 10–11.

2. Peter Leithart, *Wise Words* (Franklin, TN: Legacy Communications, 1995), 99.

3. 1 Corinthians 1:13

4. Ephesians 4:4–6

5. John Murray, "The Nature and Unity of the Church," *Collected Writings, Volume 2: Systematic Theology* (Carlisle, PA: The Banner of Truth Trust, 1977), 334.

6. Ephesians 5:25–33

7. Revelation 19:7

3 *The Visibility of the Church*

1. "A Service of Song," in *Favorite Poems of Emily Dickinson*, Eds. Mabel Loomis Todd and T. W. Higginson (New York: Avenel, 1978), 76.

2. Peter J. Leithart, *The Kingdom and the Power* (Phillipsburg, NJ: P&R, 1993), 144.

3. *Confession of Faith*, Chapter 25, sections 1 and 2

4. Emphasis added

5. Philip Edgcumbe Hughes, *A Commentary on the Epistle to the Hebrews* (Grand Rapids, MI: Eerdmans, 1977), 418. Earlier in his examination of this word, Hughes states that "there seems to be no justification for treating [the term] as a synonym for the church universal—true though it may be that forsaking the local assembly is a step toward withdrawal from the church in its totality."

6. Emphasis added

7. Alexis de Tocqueville, *Democracy in America*. Ed. and abridged by Richard D. Heffner (New York: Penguin, 1984), 193.

8. Richard F. Lovelace, *Dynamics of Spiritual Life: An Evangelical Theology of Renewal* (Downers Grove, IL: InterVarsity, 1979), 167–8.

9. Emphasis added

10. Jonathan Edwards, "An Essay on the Trinity," *Treatise on Grace and Other Posthumously Published Writings*, ed. Paul Helm (Cambridge:

James Clarke, 1971), 118. Quoted in John Piper, *The Pleasures of God* (Portland, OR: Multnomah, 1991), 44.

11. Emphasis added

12. Emphasis added

13. Emphasis added

14. Emphasis added

15. C. S. Lewis, *The Screwtape Letters* (New York: Macmillan, 1982), 12–13.

4 *The Business of the Church*

1. O. Palmer Robertson, Unpublished Paper, "Kingdom and the Church: Toward a Reformational View of Total Christian Involvement," 1.

2. George Eldon Ladd, *A Theology of the New Testament* (Grand Rapids, MI: Eerdmans, 1974), 119.

3. Louis Berkof, *Systematic Theology* (Grand Rapids, MI: Eerdmans, 1939), 569–70.

4. John Murray, "The Church and Mission," *Collected Writings, Volume 1: The Claims of Truth* (Carlisle, PA: Banner of Truth Trust, 1976), 250.

5. The office of the deacon in the Church needs a much larger development than can be given here. However, it is enough to say that the very existence of the office created by the apostles proves the point that in the apostles' mind was a self-conscious withdrawing from certain spheres and embracing of others in order to maintain the integrity of the Church's mission. "Christ's saving work not only overcomes the alienation between sinful

humans and the holy God, but also sets in motion antidotes to the 'toxic waste' of that alienation—financial want, sickness, sorrow, suffering, hostility, and death. Although these two aspects of God's salvation and the church's ministry cannot be separated from each other, the apostles recognized that they had to be distinguished from each other. Therefore, each ministry of God's grace was entrusted to leaders who could give it their undivided attention." Dennis E. Johnson, *The Message of Acts in the History of Redemption* (Phillipsburg, NJ: P&R, 1997), 90.

The question also needs to be asked as to whether the diaconal office has ever really embraced its calling. Moses told Israel in Deuteronomy 15:4 that, "there should be no poor among you." The phrase "among you" is significant because it refers not to the world at large but to the unique community of God's people. But the community of God's people extends further than one's own particular congregation. It appears that a decidedly "proactive" view of deacons is favored in the Scripture rather than a purely "reactive" conception. If a church diaconate ever truly embraced that mission, what would be the result? It is our view that the impact would be dramatic, *precisely* because the church focused her responsibilities.

6. We are not suggesting that diaconal responsibilities never overlap with activities in the world. There is a gray area here. However the Scriptural witness is clear that deacons must be responsible to communing members in their own parish first, then, using Godly wisdom, assist believers as they extend charity to those outside of the church.

7. G. I. Williamson, *The Shorter Catechism, Volume 1: Questions 1-38* (Phillipsburg, NJ: Presbyterian and Reformed Publishing, 1970), 39.

8. John Armstrong, gen. ed., *The Coming Evangelical Crisis* (Chicago: Moody, 1996), 22.

9. Ronald Wallace, *Calvin's Doctrine of the Word and Sacrament* (Edinburgh: Scottish Academic Press, 1995), 240–1.

10. Shorter Catechism, Question 94.

11. John Murray, *Redemption: Accomplished and Applied* (Grand Rapids, MI: Eerdmans, 1955), 169.

12. Shorter Catechism, Question 96.

13. Eugene Peterson, *Working the Angles* (Grand Rapids, MI: Eerdmans, 1987), 150.

5 *The Identity of the Church*

1. Leviticus 26:12

2. John Calvin, *Sermons on the Epistle to the Ephesians* (1562; reprint, Carlisle, Pa.: Banner of Truth Trust, 1975) quoted in James Montgomery Boice, *Ephesians: An Expositional Commentary* (Grand Rapids, MI: Baker), pg.43.

3. D. Martyn Lloyd-Jones, *God's Ultimate Purpose: An Exposition of Ephesians 1* (Grand Rapids, MI: Baker, 1978), 431.

4. Philippians 1:21

5. Lloyd-Jones, *Ephesians*, 432.

6. Emphasis added

7. James I. Packer, *A Quest for Godliness: The Puritan Vision of the Christian Life* (Wheaton, IL: Crossway, 1990), 299.

8. Will Metzger, *Tell the Truth* (Downers Grove: InterVarsity,

1981), 28.

9.   Ibid.

6   *The Submission of the Church*

1.   For a fuller account of Margaret Wilson's experience, see Jock
     Purves' *Fair Sunshine* (Carlisle, PA: Banner of Truth Trust, 1968),
     80–2. The book is filled with such accounts.

2.   James Bannerman, *The Church of Christ* (St. Edmonton, AB,
     Canada: Still Waters Revival, 1991), 1:188 (emphasis mine).

3.   Numbers 9:17–20, 23 (emphasis mine).

4.   Emphasis added

5.   Colossians. 1:9-12

6.   Emphasis added

7.   Church historian Mark Noll begins his work entitled *The Scandal of
     the Evangelical Mind* with these words: "The scandal of the evangelic
     mind is that there is not much of an evangelical mind." Mark A.
     Noll, *The Scandal of the Evangelical Mind* (Grand Rapids, MI:
     Eerdmans, 1994), 3.

8.   William Cunningham, *Historical Theology* (Carlisle, PA: Banner of
     Truth Trust, 1994), 1:51.

9.   Emphasis added

10. In his commentary on the Book of Philippians, J. B.
     Lightfoot observes: "It is a fact generally recognized by theologians
     of all shades of opinion, that in the language of the New
     Testament the same officer in the Church is called indifferently
     'bishop' (*episkopos*) and 'elder' or 'presbyter' (*presbuteros*)." He goes
     on to examine this fact in some detail, appealing to both

Scripture and ancient church history. See J. B. Lightfoot, *Saint Paul's Epistle to the Philippians* (Grand Rapids, MI: Zondervan, 1953), 95–9.

11. Emphasis added

12. Emphasis added

13. Emphasis added

14. The Septuagint is the Greek translation of the Old Testament. It aids in our understanding of the Greek language used in the New Testament books.

15. K. Rengstorf, Ed. Gerhard Friedrich, Trans. Geoffrey W. Bromiley, "stello," *Theological Dictionary of the New Testament* (Grand Rapids, MI: Eerdmans, 1971), 7:591–2.

16. This is exactly what took place in Acts 15. See vv. 15–18.

7 *The Love of the Church*

1. Karen Howe, "Husbands, Forget the Heroics!" *Eternity* 25, no. 12 (December 1974): 11. Quoted in Bryan Chapell, *Each for the Other: Marriage As It's Meant to Be* (Grand Rapids, MI: Baker, 1998), 59.

2. Perhaps this is an opportunity to practice what Paul said to the church in Ephesus: "Find out what pleases the Lord" (Eph. 5:10).

3. Emphasis added

4. Emphasis added

5. O. Hallesby, *Prayer* (Minneapolis: Augsburg, 1931), 75–6.

6. The Scriptures provide models for believers in their prayer for revival. Two examples would be Psalm 85 and Isaiah 63:15–64:12.

7. Emphasis added

8 *The Future of the Church*

1. *Confession of Faith*, Chapter 26, sections 2 (all)

2. C. S. Lewis, *The Weight of Glory and Other Addresses*, (New York: Macmillan Publishing Company, 1949), 19.

3. Matthew 25:44–46

4. D. Martyn Lloyd-Jones, *Studies In The Sermon on the Mount, Volume 2*, (Grand Rapids: Eerdmans, 1960), 64-5.

5. Revelation 4:8

6. It must be said here, however, that this desire to wear one's best as we gather as believers has very little to do with the actual quality of the clothes the individual chooses to wear there. The issue at hand is whether the clothes one wears are indeed their "best" clothes. One could imagine a homeless man attending public worship with believers in clothes that are actually his best, but to the eyes of others look as if they were not. Perhaps this is the embarrassing reason why more homeless men and women do not attend our worship services. This is to the Church's shame.

7. Donald Macleod, *A Faith To Live By*, (Fearn, Ross-shire: Christian Focus Publications, 1998), 298-9.

8. Donald Macleod, *Faith*, 299.

9. Ibid, 300.

10. J. R. R. Tolkien, *The Return of the King* (New York: Ballantine, 1973), 377–8.